T0311767

Cambridge Elements ≡

Elements in Travel Writing
edited by
Nandini Das
University of Oxford
Tim Youngs
Nottingham Trent University

ECO-TRAVEL

Journeying in the Age of the Anthropocene

Michael Cronin
Trinity College Dublin

CAMBRIDGE
UNIVERSITY PRESS

CAMBRIDGE
UNIVERSITY PRESS

University Printing House, Cambridge CB2 8BS, United Kingdom

One Liberty Plaza, 20th Floor, New York, NY 10006, USA

477 Williamstown Road, Port Melbourne, VIC 3207, Australia

314–321, 3rd Floor, Plot 3, Splendor Forum, Jasola District Centre,
New Delhi – 110025, India

103 Penang Road, #05–06/07, Visioncrest Commercial, Singapore 238467

Cambridge University Press is part of the University of Cambridge.

It furthers the University's mission by disseminating knowledge in the pursuit of
education, learning, and research at the highest international levels of excellence.

www.cambridge.org
Information on this title: www.cambridge.org/9781108823340
DOI: 10.1017/9781108913904

First published 2022

A catalogue record for this publication is available from the British Library.

ISBN 978-1-108-82334-0 Paperback
ISSN 2632-7090 (online)
ISSN 2632-7082 (print)

Eco-Travel

Journeying in the Age of the Anthropocene

Elements in Travel Writing

DOI: 10.1017/9781108913904
First published online: February 2022

Michael Cronin
Trinity College Dublin

Author for correspondence: Michael Cronin, CRONINM8@tcd.ie

Abstract: Human encounters with the natural world are inseparable from the history of travel. Nature, as fearsome obstacle, a wonder to behold or a source of therapeutic refuge, is bound up with the story of human mobility. Stories of this mobility give readers a sense of the diversity of the natural world, how they might interpret and respond to it and how human preoccupations are a help or a hindrance in maintaining biocultural diversity. Travel writing has constantly shaped how humans view the environment from foreign adventures to flight-shaming. If much of modern travel writing has been based on ready access to environmentally damaging forms of transport how do travel writers deal with a practice that is destroying the world they claim to cherish? *Eco-Travel* explores human travel encounters with the environment over the centuries and asks: what is the future for travel writing in the age of the Anthropocene?

Keywords: travel writing, ecology, environmental humanities, mobility, anthropocene

ISBNs: 9781108823340 (PB), 9781108913904 (OC)
ISSNs: 2632-7090 (online), 2632-7082 (print)

Contents

1 The Nature of the World

Introduction

Nobody lives on Henderson Island in the South Pacific. An isolated and uninhabited coral atoll, it was designated an UNESCO Heritage Site in 1988 in recognition of its unique ecological character. It is the kind of remote ecological island Eden that has enthused the imagination of travellers for centuries (Grove 1995). Remote, inaccessible, different, alluring, Henderson Island has also gained the unenviable distinction of having the highest density of human-made debris on the planet. Almost 38 million pieces of plastic have been found on its coastline and each day that passes brings 13,000 new pieces ashore. In the North Pacific, Midway Island, one of the most remote islands in the world, lies at the centre of the Great Pacific Garbage Patch, a huge concentration of plastic litter covering a surface that is almost three times the size of France (Hoffman 2019, 195–8). Islands that formerly offered visions of unexampled environmental plenty are now witness to unparalleled ecological devastation. Travelling there now is less about establishing an inventory of delight than drawing up a catalogue of loss. More specifically, is there a sense in which the inventories of delight have prefigured the catalogues of loss? How have travel and writing about travel contributed to the ecological degradation of the planet? Conversely, what role has travel writing played in making readers aware of the climate emergency and the need to promote sustainable forms of engagement with a planet in crisis? To begin to answer these questions we need to reflect on how travellers' perceptions of the environment have changed over the centuries.

On Easter Sunday 1245, Friar John of Pian de Carpini set out from Lyons on a journey that would take him on an uncharted expedition into the vast Mongol empire. On his return from a two-year odyssey that included the coronation ceremony of Kuyuk Khan, the grandson of Genghis Khan, he penned an account of his travels, beginning: 'There is towards the east, a land which is called Mongol, or Tartary.' He does not begin with himself. There is no mention of history. Pope Innocent IV, who sent him on this mission to the Mongol court, is wholly absent from the opening sentences. The immediate context for the voyage was geographical and environmental. Friar John lays out the territories and seas situated on the cardinal points of the empire. He then describes what manner of country is inhabited by those he calls 'Tartars':

> In some parts it is full of mountains, and in other places plain and smooth ground, but everywhere sandy and barren, neither is the hundredth part of it fruitful. For it cannot bear fruit unless it be moistened with river waters which are very rare in this country . . . Though this land is unfruitful, yet it is very commodious for the raising of cattle. In certain places there are some small

groves of trees growing, but otherwise it is altogether destitute of woods.
Therefore, the emperor, and his noblemen and all others warm themselves,
and cook their meat, with fires made of the dung of oxen and horses.

(John of Pian de Carpini 1929, 27)

First things first. What the reader needs to know from the outset is what of kind
of environment sustains this expanding empire. Our attention is immediately
drawn to the fragility of the natural life-support systems – the rare river waters,
the scarcity of trees – and the dependency of Mongols on other species (oxen,
horses) for the resources that allow them to stay warm and cook their food. The
Franciscan friar brings back knowledge about the modes and manners of the
Mongols and the political ambitions of their ruler but he starts with the basics,
the non-human world, that enable any form of human society or culture to
emerge.

Eight centuries later, the priorities have remained unchanged. As the World
Wildlife Fund (WWF) *Living Planet Report* points out: '[B]iodiversity plays
a critical role in providing food, fibre, water, energy, medicines and other
genetic materials.' Furthermore, 'nature underpins all dimensions of human
health and contributes on non-material levels – inspiration and learning, physical and psychological experiences and shaping our identities – that are central
to quality of life and cultural integrity' (Almond, Grooten and Petersen 2020, 6).
The data that feed the WWF conclusions are collected all over the world and it is
this 'travelling' science that allows for global observations. The main message,
echoing the earlier sentiments of Friar John, is that there is no humanity without
a planet to sustain it. Equally, however, there is no understanding of this
conclusion if we do not reflect on how human mobility has both contributed
to the current environmental predicament and helped us make sense of it. Travel
writing as a continuous record of humans on the move and their engagement
with the environment provides privileged insights into changing perceptions of
the non-human world. It has also been a powerful contributing factor to how that
world has been both made and unmade by humans.

Treating travel writing as a formative environmental force means moving
away from any notion of 'nature' as a referent for an objective material
phenomenon. Raymond Williams argued in *Keywords* that 'nature is perhaps
the most complex word in the language' (Williams 1983, 219). Part of that
complexity is to do with changing attitudes to the natural world that have
culminated in Bill McKibbens' appropriately entitled work, *The End of
Nature* (1989). McKibbens' argument is that humans have so fully domesti-
cated the earth and changed natural processes that it is no longer feasible to
discuss nature as something apart, leading a separate existence (McKibbens
1990; see also Coates 1998). The natural world is profoundly shaped by human

agency and human agency is, in turn, deeply influenced by the constructs it uses to interpret or understand that world. These constructs are both revealed by and elaborated through the medium of writing about travel. In this Element, we will be considering three phases in the evolving relationship between travel writing and the environment. The first phase will involve looking at how travel has historically shaped perceptions of the environment understood as the natural, non-human world affected by human activity. In the second phase, we will move to examine the role of travel writing in raising a general awareness of the climate crisis and how the genre has responded. The third phase will investigate future scenarios for travel writing in the age of human-induced climate change and potential ecological collapse. The core thesis is that travel writing is not peripheral but central to human engagement with the environment. Whether considering the ends of travel or the 'End of Travel', no reflection on our shared environmental futures can do without a close examination of the history and representations of human mobility found in the pages of travel accounts.

Climate

The anonymous author of the *Journal of the First Voyage of Vasco da Gama*, a voyage that took place between 1497 and 1499, knew that no movement is possible without the assistance of the natural world. Nothing moves without the wind and there is no life without fresh water. Rounding the Cape of Good Hope, the Portuguese scribe notes that the vessels favoured by a strong stern wind:

> were able to overcome the currents which we had feared might frustrate our plans. Henceforth it pleased God in His mercy to allow us to make Headway! We were not again driven back. May it please Him that it be thus always [si]!
>
> (Ley 1947, 10)

Later, as the ships track along the east coast of Africa, they drop anchor close to the islets of São Jorge and remain there for three days, 'in the hope that God would grant us a favourable wind' (19). In his representation of the larger forces that determine the success of their voyage, the Portuguese traveller points to two key agents: Nature and God. However, the relationship between the two is not one of equals. A favourable wind is God's gift to give. The sea currents are at the mercy of divine goodwill. The environment is anthropomorphised as the instrument of a supra-human agent who allows his emotions to dictate climate outcomes. Richard L. Gregory in *Mind in Science* describes this form of thinking as mythological, prescientific, the notion that lightning in the heavens is not a physical phenomenon but the visible trace of the anger of the gods (Gregory 1984, 7–38). It is also, however, the expression of the idea that the natural world is subordinate to divine sovereignty. It follows that, if humans in the Christian tradition are made in the image of God, it is only natural that they, too, should have a share in this subordination. The Book of Genesis provides a rationale that is fraught with consequence:

> So God created man in his own image, in the image of God created he him; male and female created he them.
>   And God blessed them, and God said unto them, Be fruitful, and multiply, and replenish the earth, and subdue it: and have dominion over the fish of the sea, and over the fowl of the air, and over every living thing that moveth upon the earth. (Gen.1: 27, 28)

The author of the *Journal* repeatedly acknowledges that he and his fellow travellers are wholly at the mercy of natural forces, but the plea for divine mediation suggests that there are limits to these environmental powers. The all-too-human agency of an all-powerful spiritual being and the associated human privilege authorised by scripture mean that the environment is as much an object to be controlled as a force to be feared. The consequences for species other than humans become clear as the Portuguese approach Seal Island near modern-day Cape Town in South Africa: 'One day, when we approached this island for our amusement, we counted among large and small ones [seals], 3,000, and we fired among them with our bombards from the sea' (Ley 1947, 9). On the same island, Vasco da Gama's chronicler notes that there were birds as 'big as ducks' that could not fly. These birds, in reality Cape Penguins, provide more opportunities for slaughter: 'These birds, of whom we killed as many as we chose, are called *fotilicaios*, and they bray like asses' (9). If the exercise of dominion in Genesis is a global project involving sovereignty 'over every living thing that moveth upon the earth', then it is less than surprising that travel accounts should provide a graphic illustration of what that subjugation on a planetary scale might look like. The world as it unfolds for the Western traveller provides a seemingly endless backdrop for the exercise of that dominion.

The sense of Adamic entitlement does not, however, make travellers less aware of environmental reciprocity. When Pero Vaz de Caminha wrote to his king in 1500 about the Portuguese discovery of Brazil, he concluded the penultimate paragraph of his letter by claiming that 'the air of the country is very healthful, fresh and as temperate as Entre Douro e Minho; we have found the two climates alike at this season' (Ley 1947, 59). When de Caminha comments on the health, cleanliness and beauty of the indigenous Tupis, he states that '[t]he air in which they are nurtured makes them what they are' (52). At one level, what he is engaging in is the kind of climatic comparison that will reach maturity in the Humboldtian ecological vison of the nineteenth century, providing an important stimulus and source of data for the emergence of a global environmental awareness. A precondition of that awareness is movement, the making of observations from different parts of the globe that is the staple of travel writing, with different emphases, throughout its history. There is no comparison without displacement, as Humboldt himself will later so graphically illustrate.

At another level, de Carminha is positing a physical and moral relationship to climate. The very air they breathe – in other words, the environment they inhabit – shapes the bodies and characters of humans. The environment becomes a kind of moral force in its own right. What travellers do is reveal the influence of environment on character, suggesting that different climates produce different outcomes. Friar John in his environmental framing of his trip through Mongol territories is at pains to point out that it is a land of extremes: 'The air ... in this country is very intemperate; in the midst of summer there are great thunders and lightnings, by which many men are slain, and at the same time there falls a great abundance of snow' (John of Pian de Carpini 1929, 27–8). What he sees as the extreme behaviour of Mongols – an intolerance of other peoples and the fact that the 'slaughter of other people is accounted no matter with them' (31) – is, in a sense, only to be expected. What is striking, apart from the political hypocrisy of discounting the blood crimes of Christian Crusaders, is the firm link between climate and behaviour.

Richard H. Grove claims a growing interest in these climatic theories as European travellers came into increasing contact with peoples previously unknown. He claims that: '[S]uch contact demanded questions as to the origins and migrations of peoples over the earth, and about the origins of species in general. Climatic explanations were easily seized upon to explain cultural behaviour and differentiation' (Grove 1995, 154). The idea of climate influencing culture was readily assimilated. It was part of how humans in the West had viewed their relationship with nature since classical times. The idea originated in medical theory: '[I]n essence, conclusions were drawn by comparing various environmental factors, such as atmospheric conditions (especially the temperature, the waters and the geographical situation), with the different individuals and people characteristic of those environments and their individual and cultural characteristics' (25). If you wanted to understand a people, you began with the natural environment. A logical consequence of this theory was not lost on certain travellers even from an early period. Change the environment and the inhabitants change too.

In a *relación* from 1579, Diego de Esquivel, a Spanish official in New Spain, notes the catastrophic effects of the loss of indigenous life resulting from European conquest. He says of the native inhabitants of Mexico:

> They live less long and have more illness than formerly because the country
> was then more thickly populated with Indians who cultivated and tilled the
> land and cleared the jungles. At the present times there are great jungles and
> forests which make all the region wild, swampy and unhealthy.
>
> (de Esquivel 1905, 60)

In this dialectic of loss, the disappearance of humans impacts the environment
and the increasingly 'wild, swampy and unhealthy' state of the environment, in
turn, affects the remaining humans. If Friar John and Diego de Esquivel, three
centuries apart, share a belief in environmental agency, they are separated by the
intellectual and cultural revolution of the Renaissance. Curiosity, which had
been viewed with suspicion by clerical authorities and thinkers, became legit-
imised in the writings and philological inquiries of the thirteenth- and four-
teenth-century humanist thinkers (Greenblatt 2012). The recovery of works of
classical antiquity would provide alternative sources of enquiry and interpretation to the Christian monopoly of understanding of, among other things, the
environment, because '[t]he Renaissance had promoted a renewed interest in
the value and portrayal of the natural world' (Grove 1995, 38). Scriptural
authority was no longer sacrosanct. Humans were no longer penitents but
agents. Exploring human possibility entailed the practical imperative to explore
the world that would reveal that possibility. Increasingly, it was not what you
were told but what you *saw* that became the touchstone of credibility.

Writing

Francis Bacon in his essay 'Of Travel' (1601) argues that '[t]ravel, in the
younger sort, is a part of education, in the elder, a part of experience' (Bacon
2002, 374). Foreign travel is no longer a question of practical necessity (as was
Friar John's mission to the Mongols) but of moral imperative, part of any
citizen's duty to know the planet they inhabit. René Descartes in his *Discours
de la méthode* (1637) can only conceive of a proper education in the comple-
mentarity of books and boats:

> This is why, as soon as I reached an age which allowed me to emerge from the
> tutelage of my teachers, I abandoned the study of letters altogether, and
> resolving to study no other science than that which I could find within myself
> or else in the great book of the world, I spent the rest of my youth in travelling.
>
> (Descartes 1968, 34)

It was not simply a question of seeing, however; it was also a matter of
recording. Experience was valueless if not committed to paper. Travel, to
have any worth, demanded to be written down. Descartes' metaphor is telling.
The reader has to get out of the study to see the world, but the world only

becomes legible as a 'book'. For Bacon, whether travel is by sea or by land, writing must always shadow movement:

> It is a strange thing, that in sea voyages, where there is nothing to be seen, but sky and sea, men should make diaries; but in land travel, wherein so much is to be observed, for the most part they omit it; as if chance were fitter to be registered, than observation. Let diaries, therefore, be brought in use.
>
> (Bacon 2002, 375)

Reading the great book of the world requires its own kind of literacy. What to look out for, what to dwell on, what to leave out will inform how travellers engage with the world. Equally, however, it will determine how they write their own great books of the world, what gets left in, what is left out. For Bacon, what gets left out is apparent in his dismissive comment 'that in sea voyages . . . there is nothing to be seen'. The entire natural history of seas and oceans is held to be nothing of account. It is the passive backdrop to a narrative void.

This was not the view of another Englishman who had held positions at Court in an earlier time, Sir Walter Raleigh. In his *Discoverie of the Large, Rich and Beautiful Empire of Guyana* (written in 1596), Raleigh is at pains to describe the natural features and locations of the rivers and seas he encounters on his expedition to Guyana. In his description of his travelling, the environment appears in two guises, as resource and as agent. If the Renaissance invitation was to go out and discover the world, political, military and financial impera-tives increasingly meant rulers were keen to turn curiosity into cash. Description becomes a prelude to appropriation as the natural world is mined both lexically and literally for resources. Raleigh details the vegetable, animal and mineral resources of his Caribbean base before describing the makeup of its peoples:

> This island of Trinidad hath the form of a sheephook, and is but narrow; the north part is very mountainous; the soil is very excellent, and will bear sugar, ginger, or any other commodity that the Indies yield. It hath store of deer, wild porks, fruit, fish, and fowl; it hath also for bread sufficient maize, cassavi, and of those roots and fruits which are common everywhere in the West Indies. It hath divers beasts which the Indies have not; the Spaniards confessed that they found grains of gold in some of the rivers; but they having a purpose to enter Guiana, the magazine of all rich metals, cared not to spend time in the search thereof any further. (Raleigh 1848, 4)

Raleigh's inventory is not innocent. The main purpose of the expedition is to enter Guyana and access its fabled 'rich metals', but his itemising of the animals to be found on Trinidad and of the crops that may be cultivated there suggests the ready instrumentalisation of the non-human world he finds on the Caribbean island. Trinidad is overlaid with an extractivist grid ('the soil is very excellent, and will bear sugar, ginger, or any other commodity'). The grid sets the context in the wider region for the emergence of what Donna Haraway refers to as the 'Plantationocene', 'the devastating transformation of diverse kinds of human-tended farms, pastures, and forests into extractive and enclosed plantations, relying on slave labor and other forms of exploited, alienated, and usually spatially transported labor' (Haraway 2015, 162).

By converting distant landscapes into extractivist potential, travel accounts involved paying a close attention to these landscapes to see what they might yield. They were less forthcoming, initially, with what the consequences of massive, capital-intensive, colonial intervention might be for native peoples, the enslaved and the environment. In much the same way as radical bohemia prospects urban possibilities for real-estate tycoons through the process of gentrification, travel writing in the Age of Exploration revealed the global extent of extractivist possibility by opening up new territories to the appropria-tive gaze of missionaries and merchants. When Vasco da Gama arrives in Calicut in India, he tells two messengers from the local ruler that he has come 'in search of Christians and of spices' (Ley 1947, 27), but it was *spices*, not Christians, that were in short supply back home.

Emphasising the environment as resource runs the risk, however, of denying the environment agency in travel writing from the early modern period. Raleigh, for example, is acutely aware of how his own ability to move forward with his plans is critically determined by the agentive possibilities of the natural world. In his Address to the Reader, Raleigh attempts to justify the ultimate failure of his expedition to Guyana:

> [W]hen we passed any branch of the river to view the land within, and stayed from our boats but six hours, we were driven to wade to the eyes at our return; and if we attempted the same the day following, it was impossible either to ford it, or to swim it, both by reason of the swiftness, and also for that the borders were so pestered with fast woods, as neither boat nor man could find place either to land or to embark; for in June, July, August, and September it is impossible to navigate any of those rivers; for such is the fury of the current, and there are so many trees and woods overflown, as if any boat but touch upon any tree or stake it is impossible to save any one person therein.
>
> (Raleigh 1848, lxix)

The principal obstacle to his success is less Spanish hostility than natural resistance. Much of the *Discoverie* is given over to Raleigh's attempting to understand the nature, location and direction of the rivers in Guyana and to how he and his companions try to overcome the environmental barriers put in their path.

Raleigh's political opponents also understand that the environment has agency. Berreo, the senior Spanish official on the island of Trinidad who is held captive by Raleigh, describes his own attempts to penetrate the Guyana interior and how he was thwarted not only by the opposition of indigenous groups but by the difficulty and dangers of the terrain. When Berreo attempts to dissuade the English adventurer from embarking for Guyana, his first argument is to invoke the perils of the natural world: 'And first he delivered that I could not enter any of the rivers with any bark or pinnace, or hardly with any ship's boat, it was so low, sandy, and full of flats, and that his companies were daily grounded in their canoes, which drew but twelve inches water' (42). Much of Raleigh's engagement, through an interpreter, with native informants on Trinidad is to inform himself of the natural geography of Guyanese territory. In Francis Bacon's later advice to travellers, there is no mention made of the natural world, but for Raleigh and his peers, travelling is constantly in dialogue with the environment. What they can do, how far they can go, is dictated by environmental affordances. The environment as passive resource remains in tension with the environment as active agent. As a primary motive for Raleigh's travel account is to persuade his English readers of the merits of further expeditions to Guyana, he must integrate environmental agency into his narrative. If the *Discoverie* is an exercise in geographical intelligence, a writing (*graphia*) about the earth (*gē*), it also shows that, much to Raleigh's chagrin, the earth can write back. Although he is thoroughly imbued with the sense of human exceptionalism that is an integral part of the legacy of Renaissance humanism, Raleigh must contend with the limits that the non-human world presents to him on his travels and that he, in turn, communicates to his readers.

Nature/Culture

Any consideration of how travel writing has engaged with the environment raises the traditionally vexed question of nature/culture distinctions and how one is defined in relation to the other. Kate Soper contends that:

> An opposition ... between the natural and the human has been axiomatic to Western thought, and remains a supposition of all its philosophical, scientific, moral and aesthetic discourse, even if the history of these discourses is in large part a history of the differing constructions we are asked to place upon it. (Soper 1995, 38)

Paul Smethurst, for his part, notes that as knowledge of the natural world increased on a global scale, due in no small part to the popularity of travel writing, 'nature acquired symbolic weight in the politics of trade and empire, where it reinforced racial, ethnic, gender and sexual prejudices by defining what was "natural" and "unnatural", and by extension, what was "primitive" or "civilised"' (Smethurst 2013, 3; see also Crane 2019, 535–49). As Western travellers meet previously unknown peoples, assumptions are readily made about who is part of the 'natural' world and who is part of the world that is human. The writing has a dual function, description and classification. Indigenous peoples are described alongside plants, geographical features and animal species and clearly situated within an environmental continuum where they are the 'natural' emanation of their biophysical hinterland.

Pero Vaz de Caminha, detailing the first Portuguese encounter with the Tupi people, compares the indigenous inhabitants of modern-day Brazil to animals found in the wild. When Diogo Dias, crew member of one of the ships, decides to play the bagpipes to entertain a small group of Tupis, de Caminha notes: '[Y]et, though he held their attention and diverted them in that way, they soon took fright as wild things from the hills will do, and went inland' (Ley 1947, 51). When the captain invites a number of Tupi onto his ship, de Caminha sees hospitality and bed linen as a necessary part of the 'civilizing' process: 'That night they were very handsomely treated, not only in the way of food, but also to a bed with mattress and sheets, the better to tame them' (57). Coming out of this unknown wilderness, they must be wild, in need of the taming hand of the civilised Europeans. If they need domestication, it is because they know nothing of domestication: 'They do not plough or breed cattle. There are no oxen here, nor goats, sheep, fowl, nor any other animal accustomed to live with man' (56). The absence of domestic animals or any visible trace of agriculture situates the Tupis beyond the pale of settled civilisation, predicated on the subjugation of animals and human intervention in the landscape. Living off the fruits of the environment, they are readily assimilated to it, although in ways that are not uniformly negative. De Caminha baldly states that the Tupis are 'a savage, ignorant people' but qualifies his comments by asserting:

> For all which they are healthy and very clean. So that I am even surer that they are like the wild birds or animals whose feathers and hair the air makes finer than when they are domesticated, and whose bodies are as clean, as plump, and as beautiful as they could possibly be. (52)

The Portuguese scribe is clearly establishing a hierarchy where the ignorant, the savage and the untamed are of a piece with the surrounding environment. It is their 'primitive' condition that will justify their future exploitation and enslavement. As indigenous peoples are assimilated to the non-human, their treatment becomes predictably inhuman. De Caminha does, however, indicate an ambivalence towards the state of nature that will run through travel writing up to the present day.

Renaissance humanism decrees humans to be the measure of all things and what justifies this pre-eminence is that humans are not bound by the determinism of nature. It is the ability to shape nature to human purposes that constitutes the bedrock of culture. As Keith Thomas points out in *Man and the Natural World*, 'primitive' peoples were deemed to lack 'the same attributes as those in which the animals were deficient: technology, intelligible language, Christianity' (Thomas 1984, 89). De Caminha's doubts arise from the supposed benefits of culture. He cannot help noticing that, in spite of the Tupis' lack of technology, intelligible language and Christianity, 'they are of a finer, sturdier, and sleeker condition than we are for all the wheat and vegetables we eat' (Ley 1947, 56). Wheat and vegetables, the totemic products of settler civilisation, do not seem to produce better health outcomes than the nomadic consumption of 'those fruits and seeds that the earth and the trees give of themselves' (56). Closeness to the natural world, he suggests, may not be as debilitating as is often claimed.

For the vast majority of Europeans, the principal source of knowledge about lands beyond their own was travel accounts. Richard Grove notes the increasing popularity of the travel writing genre culminating in the spectacular rise in the number of titles in the eighteenth century: '[T]ravel literature was entering an extraordinary period of growth, very much in parallel with the process of territorial expansion by European maritime powers' (Grove 1995, 229). Readers' environmental awareness, especially but not only on a supra-regional scale, was determined less by what they saw and more by what they read. Their view of the natural world and the role of nature in culture would be informed by the environmental news from elsewhere. The success of the genre, albeit under the long shadow of European imperialism, was that:

> Europe was deluged with accounts of the habits, appearance, social organisation, religion, agriculture and other details of 'exotic' societies, as well as corresponding accounts of the local climate, natural productions, animals, plants, minerals, drugs, food and so on. (162)

Sight

What readers could not directly witness for themselves, they could indirectly see through the accounts, illustrations or maps of the traveller. When Martin Heidegger claimed that 'the fundamental event of the modern age is the conquest of the world as picture' (Heidegger 1977, 134), he both subverts and amplifies the authority of the word. In the premodern world, the word of scriptural or classical authority was sacrosanct. As scientific method evolves in the Renaissance, however, proof is not what you hold on authority but what you behold with your eyes. Experiments allow others to see for themselves what has been affirmed. The Copernican and Newtonian revolutions would firmly establish ocularcentrism in Western thinking. Observation became the touchstone of legitimacy in Western science and, where the eye could not see, optical instruments (microscopes, telescopes) or visual metaphors stepped in (Levin 1993). Literacy and the advent of printing further strengthened visual and spatialised perceptions of experience (Ong 2012). If seeing is believing, then travel writing in the new truth regime of scientific modernity has an even more crucial function, testing beliefs or assumptions about peoples and their environments against eyewitness reports from elsewhere. The word is both demoted by the visual and reinforced by the practical necessity of its truth claims.

As most readers are unable or unwilling to travel to distant places, they 'see' through the words of others. The consequent pressure on the travel writers themselves can be sensed in a strategic defensiveness about some of their more exotic claims. In his thirteenth-century description of the various military conquests of the Mongols, Friar John baldly asserts that they came to a 'country lying upon the ocean sea, where they found certain monsters, who in all things resembled the shape of men, saving that their feet were like the feet of an ox, and they had indeed men's heads but dog's faces' (John of Pian de Carpini 1929, 45). When Walter Raleigh, three centuries later, affirms the connection between the environmentally remote and the humanly monstrous, he is much more tentative. Describing the river system of Guyana and the distribution of various indigenous peoples, Raleigh affirms:

> Next unto Arui there are two rivers Atoica and Caura, and on that branch which is called Caura are a nation of people whose heads appear not above their shoulders; which though it may be thought a mere fable, yet for mine own part I am resolved it is true, because every child in the provinces of Aromaia and Canuri affirm the same. They are called Ewaipanoma; they are reported to have their eyes in their shoulders, and their mouths in the middle of their breasts, and that a long train of hair groweth backward between their shoulders. (Raleigh 1848, 85)

Raleigh is aware that, in the new truth regime, his claims might invite scepticism. The associations of travellers' accounts with 'mere fable', which dogs the legitimacy of the genre, must be countered. Although Raleigh himself has not met the Ewaipanoma, he seeks truth in numbers. If even the children in the provinces of Aromaia and Canuri affirm their existence, they must have seen them or known them to exist. Claims now require proofs, either direct or credible indirect evidence (even if Raleigh's faith in the credibility of the children of the region is open to its own kind of doubt).

From an environmental standpoint, the ascendancy of the visual has two major consequences. First, any claim that is made about environmental makeup or influence must be situated in eyewitness claims. They must be seen (and then described) to be believed. Second, the nature of a wider public response to environmental questions and, more specifically, to the engagement with the natural world, will be determined by the form of that visualisation. In the case of the first consequence, the clear implication is that a global environmental awareness involves global travelling. Even the 'wilderness' must be tracked by human eye to demonstrate that it is a wilderness (see Lee 2019, 376–90). Travel writers may later come to scorn the environmental depredation of mass tourism, but the visual truth regime of a particular kind of travel writing means that no part of the planet can remain inviolate.

In the case of the second consequence, the form of the visualisation, how travel writers choose to represent a place or landscape can critically determine their readers' reception of these places and landscapes. Diana K. Davis has coined the term 'environmental imaginary' to describe 'the constellation of ideas that groups of humans develop about a given landscape', and which are frequently transmitted through stories or narratives 'about that environment as well as how it came to be in its current state'. In the context of colonisation and empire, those who decide on such environmental representations and their meanings 'can determine who wins and who loses when that imaginary is operationalized in the form of concrete [environmental] policies and practices' (Davis 2011, 3). These imaginaries have a long shelf life, as evidenced by the contemporary branding of the west coast of Ireland as the 'Wild Atlantic Way'. The difficulty with environmental imaginaries inherited from the colonial period and given a renewed lease by versions of cultural nationalism is that stories of ecological destruction and human loss are often masked by the photo ops of the hospitality industry. As Matthew Kelly notes: '[T]he US parks might be based on notions of wilderness, and Glenveagh [National Park in Donegal, Ireland] on nineteenth-century scenic ideals, but both stem from violent acts of appropriation. The US park authorities expelled indigenous populations and later arrivals with a ruthlessness that mirrors Adair [Glenveagh's landlord]'(Kelly 2019, 137). In reality, the Wild Atlantic Way is nothing if not a long *via dolorosa* of economic dispossession (poverty, emigration) and ecological dislocation (deforestation, soil erosion, species extinction). The history of the environmental imaginary plays out as a recurrent tension between landscape as representation and landscape as commodity. Selling a landscape involves encouraging others to believe in its value. If it must be seen to be believed, it must be seen in a particular way.

The particular ways of seeing associated with travel writing have often obscured its importance for the shaping of environmental imaginaries and its role in the emergence of environmental awareness. Carl Thompson points to the anachronisms that have marginalised travel writing's contribution to wider scientific and societal debates:

> Travel writing today is generally viewed as a minor literary genre, read principally for personal amusement. Eighteenth- and nineteenth-century voyages and travels, however, were certainly a very popular, widely selling form (far more so than modern travel writing), yet, in the age of Cook, Darwin, Mungo Park, Arthur Young, William Gilpin and many others, the genre was simultaneously a vital medium for debate and dissemination across a broad range of disciplines and discourses. (Thompson 2017, 135)

Prior to the early nineteenth century, the assumption was that a reader of a travel account could expect to be informed on a range of topics and these would be grounded in verifiable fact rather than mere opinion (Turner 2001; Leask 2002; Jarvis 2012). The inclusive, interdisciplinary nature of a genre that was taken to be a serious contributor to intellectual discussion owed part of its prestige to the importance of the knowledge function of the writing in the early modern period. The point was education, not escape. That travel writing could do this so successfully in the area of environmental knowledge until well into the nineteenth century was partly a result of a more general lack of professionalisation of scientific disciplines. James Secord has argued that a division between popular and specialist science 'is inappropriate to understanding a period when people differing in gender, rank and depth of expertise not only talked about science but in so doing contributed directly to its making' (Secord 2006, 132). Distinctions between amateurs and specialists, disciplinary demarcations, were considerably more fluid than they would subsequently become (Turner 2014, 231–380). One consequence is that women travellers could use the authority and (relative) inclusiveness of the travel writing to contribute to environmental knowledge and debates. The status of travel writing and the dependence of science on a network of local informants meant that natural history did not become an exclusively male prerogative. Through the medium of travel, 'women were not invariably positioned on the outside of key knowledge networks' (Thompson 2017, 139).

Interiority

From the outset of her *Letters from the Island of Teneriffe, Brazil, the Cape of Good Hope, and the East Indies* (1777) Jemima Kindersley is explicit in both her purpose and methodology. In the opening paragraph of her account, addressing her anonymous correspondent, she declares: 'I now begin to fulfil the promise I made, of giving you a particular account of whatsoever I should observe, either in the course of my voyage, or during my residence in India' (Kindersley 1777, 1). As she travels from the Canary Islands to Brazil to South Africa and on to India, she remains true to her word, offering information on the history, politics, religion and geography of the territories she visits. Journeying in the 1760s, she respects the Baconian injunction to rely on observation and the evidence of the eye. In the Dutch Cape colony, she prefaces her description of the indigenous people by declaring: 'I have purposely deferred giving you any account of the natives of this country, the Hottentots, till I could be assured that the strange accounts I heard of them were true; my eyes have convinced me, that some of them are, and others I have from good authority' (68).

What is notable in the passage is the 'I' (repeated three times) in eyewitness. The first-person pronoun indicates a profound shift in sensibility in the eighteenth century from objective chronicle to subjective witness. The Renaissance Human mutates into the Romantic Self and the focus moves inwards:

> In romantic travel writing, topographical description is extended into subjective relations between landscape and the mind. This brings the space of nature into the realm of psychic space, where it is connected with the traveller's mental fabrication of the natural world. The emphasis on *interiority*, especially in encounters with the natural sublime, contrasts with the empiricism of the museum order and the distancing and framing of the picturesque. (Smethurst 2013, 153 [emphasis in original])

Kindersley's account is marked by the growing emphasis on interiority, the greater attention to 'self-in-society' mirrored by an increased preoccupation with 'self-in-nature' (Kindersley 1777, 54). Kindersley tells her reader not only what she knows but also what she feels. The natural world is not there only to be described. It is there to be experienced. The narrative function of the travel writer becomes more explicit as she looks to bring to life the internal world of sentiment alongside the external world of object and event. Kindersley combines features of the 'modes and manners' narrative with its objective language of topographical and statistical description and those of the 'sentimental' narrative that detail subjective responses to place (Elsner and Rubiés 1999, 1–56). The environment is as much a matter of personal encounter as it is of physical description.

What results is a hybrid form of evidence, both grounded in observation, one part phenomenological, one part technical. In a letter from Madras in southern India, Kindersley notes that the 'heat here is excessive' (Kindersley 1777, 67); this is how she directly experiences the climate. In a later letter from Calcutta, she gives a more clinical description of the harmful effects of the sun on English colonists. One slow killer is 'bile in the stomach', which Kindersley explains as follows: '[T]he intense heat relaxes the coats of the stomach so as to prevent digestion, which occasions much illness, and oft-times death' (Kindersley 1777, 85). Echoing the Hippocratic concern for the influence of climate on health (Grove 1995, 13), Kindersley uses her subject position to explore a gender dimension to the climate question. She notes that '[i]t is frequently said, though very unjustly, that this climate never kills the English ladies' (Kindersley 1777, 85). Acknowledging that 'women do not often die of violent fevers as men', she argues that this 'is no wonder, as we [women] live more temperately, and expose ourselves less in the heat of the day' (85). For Kindersley, however, the fact remains that 'most English women labour under the oppression of weak nerves, slow fevers and bile', the combined effects of which destroy 'the roses on the cheeks of the young and beautiful' and give 'them a pale yellow complexion' (86). Kindersley is reporting on what she sees and explaining it in terms of the medical knowledge she has at her disposal. What is telling is how the natural world is increasingly a human construct. In other words, a climatic factor such as heat is framed in terms of the gendered pressures on personal appearance and the physical survival of colonists. The effects of both the scientific explanation and the human concerns are to move the natural world into the background. The more that human reason can account for its effects, the more malleable it becomes to human intervention.

If 'travel writing in the eighteenth century was the primary vehicle for informing the public at large about new discoveries in the natural world' (Smethurst 2013, 6), it would also offer its Western readers suggestions for appropriate responses to this natural world. Travelling by river from Calcutta, Kindersley comes to the fort town of Mongheir and describes the surrounding area:

> The country about is remarkably fertile, beautiful and healthy. About two miles distant is a house on the top of a very high hill, which commands a vast extent of country, with everything that can form a romantic and delightful prospect. On the one side, the Ganges, with the near and distant rocks; on the other, the fort, numberless hills and valleys, with woods, villages, corn-fields, and gardens; single houses and mosques scattered here and there; elephants, buffalos, camels, and all kinds of cattle, which, with the people, form a moving landscape of great variety, in miniature. (Kindersley 1777, 91)

She notes that it 'is a delightful retreat for the commanding officer of the troops' (91). The view from a height allows the scene to be framed. In the terms of the picturesque, it is a 'prospect'. In terms of emotional impact, it is 'romantic'. Following Charles Jencks' distinctions between three kinds of material nature, we have nature untended ('woods'), nature tended ('corn-fields') and nature intended ('gardens') (Jencks 2005, 389). There are natural formations ('rocks') and human constructions ('houses and mosques'), human species ('people') and non-human species ('elephants, buffalos, camels'). The landscape has the necessary picturesque qualities of singular offerings (the distinct features that underpin 'the variety') and the demonstrable capacity to affect the viewer (the artfully ambiguous 'moving landscape'). This view from a distance means that everything can be seized 'in miniature'. The position of the viewer is magnified, the position of the viewed reduced. The natural world and the traces of human interaction with the environment are captured in this panoptic gaze, which situates the viewer close to the site of power. The house on the hill is where we find the 'commanding officer of the troops'. From the command post of colonial observation and control, the natural world and the native peoples inhabiting it are scaled back to an animated vignette. Seeing is more than believing (in imperial might). It is belittling.

Mary Louise Pratt has described how frequently this form of visual capture from the commanding heights features in Western travel accounts from the colonial period, and she argues that it continues into the present: 'In contemporary travel accounts, the monarch-of-all-I-survey scene gets repeated, only now from the balconies of big hotels in third-world cities' (Pratt 1992, 216). From an environmental perspective, the equation between distance and control implies that the more that aesthetics and politics conspire to frame and abstract the natural world, the more difficult it becomes to disentangle representations of nature from practices that are deeply damaging to environmental sustainability.

The 'Monarchs' may be removed, or may seek to remove themselves, from the consequences of their actions, but it is immeasurably more difficult for 'elephants, buffalos, camels' and (subject) 'people' to move out of what Naomi Klein has called the 'sacrifice zones' of environmental extractivism (Klein 2014, 310). If travel writing for several centuries bore the burden of environmental representation for many readers in the Global North, the inescapable consequence was that there was no nature separate from culture, no means of apprehending a prior environmental reality separate from specific human designs.

John Locke praises those travel writers who 'expose themselves to the Dangers of the vast ocean ... whilst the rest of Mankind, in their accounts, without stirring a foot, compass the Earth and the Seas, visit all Countries, and converse with all Nations' (Locke 1704, lxxiii). The travel account for the English philosopher is discovery by proxy, a cognitive mapping of the world, a key node in the knowledge network of modernity. The difficulty was how to stop scope from promoting – not preventing – disconnection. In other words, as the vision of the traveller became more global, with its promise to 'compass the Earth and the Seas, visit all Countries, and converse with all Nations', how would the view from afar not transform into control from above? If the world were shrinking for the Lockean armchair traveller, what was to prevent these moving landscapes 'in miniature' from becoming the playthings of powerful mercantilist and imperial interests?

The writers could go anywhere but so too could the troops, traders, missionaries and miners. In the next section, we will see how travel writing would come to challenge environmental destructiveness, but here we want to consider how the appropriative standpoint of the imperial gaze fed into two developments fraught with ecological consequence: Heidegger's understanding of the conquest of the world as picture and the rise of scenic tourism.

Marguerite Blessington on her way into Naples orders her postilion to stop on the brow of a steep hill so that she may 'gaze on the beautiful panorama' before her (Blessington 1839, 191–2). She wants a good view but what constituted a good view was, of course, constructed not given. You had to be trained to look at the natural world in specific ways. Gazing was, in effect, an intensely curated form of seeing. Richard Payne Knight makes this explicit in *An Analytical Inquiry into the Principles of Taste*:

> The spectator having his mind enriched with the embellishments of the painter and the poet, applies them, by the spontaneous association of ideas, to the natural objects presented to his eye, which thus acquire ideal and imaginary beauties. (Payne Knight 1806, 154)

The mind of Marguerite Blessington was particularly enriched by the works of three painters, Nicolas Poussin, Claude Lorrain and Salvator Rosa. The view from on high was a basic rule in the artwork of Claude Lorrain (Lipska 2017, 56–7). Blessington was also sensitive, as were so many travel writers of her generation, to the aesthetic strictures of William Gilpin in his *Three Essays: On Picturesque Beauty; On Picturesque Travel; and on Sketching Landscapes: To Which is Added a Poem, On Landscape Painting* (1794). Paul Smethurst has described how notions of the picturesque and the Romantic came to deeply inform the writing of even the most sober scientific travel accounts of the eighteenth and nineteenth centuries (Smethurst 2013, 6). Not surprisingly, the influences were more obvious and palpable in travel writing that was not directed at what were seen, in the nineteenth century, as increasingly specialist audiences. The very titles of two of Marguerite Blessington's works – *The Idler in Italy* (1839–40) and *The Idler in France* (1841–42) – point to the emergence of a class of traveller who considers travel a form of leisure rather than a trial of endurance. The relationship to the environment is less about grappling with the unknown than about appropriately framing the familiar. One of the devices that fashionable travellers carried with them was a Claude glass, described by Aneta Lipska as follows:

> Carried in hand, it was used to examine the landscape with one's back to the real view. The device was a dark-tinted convex mirror which not only condensed and diminished the reflected piece of scenery (thus abstracting it from its surroundings), but also reduced and simplified the colours and tonal range of scenes, giving them, in consequence, a painterly quality characteristic of Claude Lorrain. (Lipska 2017, 59)

It is telling that the travellers have their back to the landscape. With their view mediated by an optical device, they are no longer obliged to see directly what they would prefer to *see* indirectly. The natural world is 'condensed and diminished' so it can be captured in a pictorial grid. The environment is no longer that which surrounds; it is that which succumbs.

Consumption

As the picturesque references classical images of a rural arcadia and Romanticism radically shifts appropriate destinations for travel – from the urban centres to the untamed periphery – the natural world itself, as much as the resources it contains, becomes an object of consumption. Travel in the form of scenic tourism emphasises this detachment from the environment. Rising incomes from the Industrial Revolution, the gradual introduction of legislation covering paid leave, the arrival of steam power and the construction of the railways and innovations in the travel industry (Thomas Cook's system of vouchers) all led to an unprecedented expansion of the number of people engaged in travel for non-utilitarian purposes (Urry and Larsen 2011, 31–48). Typically, travellers sought to escape cities to head for the countryside or the seaside. The growing phenomenon of urbanisation in the nineteenth century meant that larger numbers of people no longer had direct experience of living in a non-urban natural world. The inhabitants of the countryside, as if viewed through a social Claude glass, became abstracted from their rural surroundings once they moved to the cities.

One consequence, as Raymond Williams has argued, was that around the notion of the 'country' has 'gathered the idea of a natural way of life: of peace, innocence, and simple virtue' (Williams 1973, 1). The access to this rural world would become increasingly mediated through the pictorial idiom of a scenic tourism which presupposed a passive, pre-edited environment waiting to be consumed. Many travel writers in the century, of course, railed against the rise of mass tourism but this had less to do with saving the environment than with protecting class privilege (Buzard 1993). The comments of the Anglo-Irish novelist Charles Lever in *Blackwood's Magazine* were typical:

> It seems that some enterprising and unscrupulous man [Thomas Cook] has devised the project of conducting some forty or fifty persons . . . from London to Naples and back for a fixed sum. He contracts to carry them, feed them, and amuse them . . . When I first read the scheme . . . I caught at the hope that the speculation would break down. I imagined that the characteristic independence of Englishmen would revolt against a plan that reduces the traveller to the level of his trunk and obliterates every trace and trait of the individual. I was all wrong. As I write, the cities of Italy are deluged with droves of these creatures. (cited in Fussell 1980, 40)

The difficulty for travel writers was that, in praising environments, they were also populating them. Drawing attention to the beauty of a particular natural setting could spell its end as an intact ecosystem. In this respect, Burke's notion of the sublime, which will profoundly influence both the form of travel writing and the destination of travellers, is particularly fraught with consequence. When Marguerite Blessington marvels at the Blackgang Chine on the Isle of Wight, her language is suitably exalted: 'Here were seen the works of God in all their native grandeur, the ocean in resplendent majesty, spreading its vast expanse as far as the eye could reach; unbounded' (Blessington 1822, 56). The sense of awe, scale and power invested in the scene picks up on Burke's famous formulation of the sublime:

> Whatever is fitted in any sort to excite the idea of pain and danger, that is to say, whatever is in any sort terrible, or is conversant about terrible objects, or operates in a manner analogous to terror is a source of the *sublime*, that is, it is productive of the strongest emotion which the mind is capable of feeling.
> (Burke 1767, 56 [emphasis in original])

Burke's blending of admiration and terror in his definition is clearly linked to the opening paragraph of the second part of his inquiry: 'The passion caused by the great and sublime in *nature*, when those causes operate most powerfully, is astonishment' (95, emphasis in original). Travel writing becomes a quest for those places in 'nature' that occasion these feelings of the great and the sublime. Remote, peripheral, inaccessible spots are now ardently sought; the Grand Tour of the urban centres and the sites of classical antiquity give way to the sublime spectacles afforded by nature, both domestic and foreign.

The sublime sets out a different itinerary for the traveller and the more inaccessible the site, the greater the travel writer's chances for shock and awe. As writing is generally, although not exclusively, a sharing of experience, privately encountering the sublime comes to mean publicly identifying the coordinates. In *The Idler in France*, Marguerite Blessington acknowledges this impulse to communicate the traveller's impressions:

> I never see a beautiful landscape, a noble ruin, or a glorious fane, without wishing that I could bequeath to those who will come to visit them when I shall be no more, the tender thoughts that filled my soul when contemplating them; and thus, even in death, create a sympathy. (Blessington 1841, 13)

The traveller's 'tender thoughts' may, however, lead to the repeat business of tourism and, in turn, the ecological perils of saturation.

Burke is fascinated less by the natural spectacles he sees than by the emotions they elicit in him just as Marguerite Blessington is eager to tell her readers about the subjective impressions made on her by a 'beautiful landscape'. In this Romantic embrace of the natural world, the environment becomes an external, largely visual trigger for strong emotion. It is as if, at the heart of this immersion in the raptures of the sublime, there is a potent distancing; the natural world becomes a site of personal projection, an internalised mental construct, rather than a presence with its own ontologies.

What proves problematic to this day in dealing with the legacy of the sublime is the question of how ecologically sensitive travel writing might escape the force of human projection onto the environment. As Paul Smethurst has shown, even the most empirically committed scientific travel writers who eschewed florid description for the plain prose of the analytic description could not resist the allure of Romantic tropes (Smethurst 2013, 88–108). In our own time, images of the grandeur of the natural world are frequently mobilised in campaigns to fight off ecological devastation in much the same way that the dramatic cinematography of David Attenborough's *Our Planet* series (2019) was used to make television audiences aware of the nature and scale of species' destruction. Using the sublime to invoke climate terror does not always, however, mean escaping the distancing strategies of anthropomorphic awe and the ensuing environmental consequences of overconsumption and despoliation.

Dipesh Chakrabarty, in an article entitled 'The Climate of History: Four Theses', has argued that when the collective actions of humans fundamentally alter the conditions of life on the planet, they move from being biological agents to becoming a geological force in their own right: 'For it is no longer a question of man having an interactive relationship with nature. This humans have always had, or at least that is how man has been imagined in a large part of what is generally called the Western tradition. Now it is being claimed that humans are a force of nature in a geological sense' (Chakrabarty 2009, 207). The travel writers, in the periods we have been discussing in this section, saw themselves mainly as environmental agents, subject to and interacting with the environment. In the age of the Anthropocene, characterised by the human ability to profoundly affect all aspects of life on the planet, it is no longer possible to speak about the 'environment' as something out there, as a negligible and dispensable externality. The environment is not external to but constitutive of what we are. Over the centuries, travel writing has been a powerful contributor to the commodification and externalisation of the environment. We will consider in the next section how travel writers would become part of a counter-movement, spelling out in graphic detail the worldwide desecration of the planet and testing new ways to write the earth.

2 The End of Nature?

Ishmael, in Hermann Melville's *Moby Dick*, is in no doubt that, 'as everyone knows, meditation and water are wedded for ever' (Melville [1851] 1967, 4). The ocean exercises a fascination for humans that excites both their desire to travel and their wish to reflect. Ishmael thinks about these associations as he prepares himself for a whaling expedition. There is an unsettling appropriateness in this human species destruction being the backdrop for Ishmael's spiritual quest. The form of the travel narrative dramatising Ishmael's encounter with the Leviathan of the deep will later be repurposed for critical engagements when meditation and water, reflection and travel are wedded. Starting with travel as a template for environmental awareness, as we move into late modernity, it is possible to see how travel writing signals not only the extent of the environmental crisis but also possible responses to that crisis. These responses range from contesting banal forms of ecological representation to seriously engaging with the nonhuman and the post-anthropocentric to taking on the legacy of mass tourism and exploring resources for more joyful entanglements with environmental futures.

Plunder

In 1948, William Vogt published *Road to Survival*. He wrote the work in the hope that humans would become aware of their increasingly ruinous relationships to the environment. They were, he argued, 'exerting a gargantuan impact upon the world of tomorrow. Disregarded, they will almost certainly smash our civilisation' (Vogt 1948, xiii). The opening pages of a book that was an unqualified success, selling millions of copies, draw directly on the scene-setting conventions of the travel account: 'The grey combers of the Tasmanian Sea raced past the ship from astern and with a slow rhythm, like that of a deep pendulum lifted its screw, to race futilely in the air' (3). The reader is then introduced to 'Maria', a Mexican woman walking along a dusty road in the Mexican state of Michoacán; Tom Cobbett, a former miner turned British Labour Party MP at his desk in Yorkshire; Jim Hanrahan, an unscrupulous American timber merchant celebrating a deal in an unnamed part of Latin America; nameless Jewish refugees in search of a homeland; Wong, a starving peasant farmer in Asia; and Joe Spencer, a scientist in his US laboratory who thinks he may have found a vaccine for malaria. The logic for the global sightseeing is made explicit by Vogt:

> All of these have one thing in common. The lot of each, from Austrian sea captain to biochemist, is completely dependent on his or her global environment, and each of them to a greater or lesser degree influences that environment. (14)

In trying to portray both the scale and the connectedness of the unfolding environmental catastrophe, Vogt uses the familiar tropes of the sentimental travel narrative – physical description, characterisation, suspense, drama and, where necessary, pathos. The first chapter opens in water and ends in mediation. It is the familiar language of travel that allows Vogt to make a case for commonality and interdependence even if his speculations on the population question make the fatal, if common, environmental assumption that all humans are born equal.

When Vogt's compatriot, Fairfield Osborn, publishes his own equally successful *Our Plundered Planet* the same year, he too reaches for the metaphor of mobility to describe the scale of the task: 'It is amazing how far one has to travel to find a person, even amongst those most widely informed, who is aware of the processes of mounting destruction that we are inflicting upon our life sources' (Osborn 1948, 194). Vogt tries to give the reader a sense of how far he has travelled to find those who are sufficiently aware of this mounting destruction:

> I have talked with trappers in Manitoba and shepherders in Patagonia; and, in between, with scientists, labor leaders, fishermen, sea captains, farmers, peasants, millionaires, presidents, cabinet ministers, diplomats, newspapermen, lumbermen, engineers etc. (Vogt 1948, xiv–xv)

Travel becomes a necessary part of environmental representation. Ecological consequence is a matter of both range and detail. Vogt needs to emphasise range to demonstrate that the environmental crisis is a global one, and he presses detail into service to show the force of certain relationships 'that every minute of every day touch the life of every man, woman and child on the face of the globe' (17).

As the world geared up materially in the postwar period for the Great Acceleration that would dramatically increase the rate of carbon emissions on the planet, two works bought and read by millions of readers warned of the ecological catastrophe that lay ahead. The ecological catastrophe is not new. It has always been known. 'Road', 'planet', 'plunder', the vocabulary of exploration, trade and pillage are the terms used to frame this environmental disaster. Travel is not only a methodology for accessing data, it is also central to the presentation and interpretation of those data. When Al Gore, almost sixty years later, reminds viewers in *An Inconvenient Truth* (2006) of the climate outcomes of postwar growth, he is endlessly on the move. The constantly shifting locations are partly to present evidence of ecological destruction, but as he moves from city to city and country to country, he is also tracking down the audiences for his environmental message.

Like Vogt and Osborn in earlier periods, the former American vice-president is not so much on the road to, as on the road for, survival. The planetary warnings become global pilgrimages to demonstrate that the 'conditions – whether material or social or even ideological – which exist among peoples in one section of the earth now have a bearing on the lives of people of far distant nations' (Osborn 1948, 34). That the mobility itself may be part of the problem is an issue we will explore in the next section, but for now, let us consider how the travel writer takes on the ecological burden of metaphor. How have travel writers in late modernity tried to make sense of the looming climate emergency?

Globes and Spheres

Preparing to land on the island of St Kilda with surveyors from the Royal Commission on Ancient and Historical Monuments of Scotland, Kathleen Jamie notes that they arrive with baggage: '[O]ut of the hold and into the dinghy came strongboxes containing satellite receivers, laptops, batteries, chargers and digital cameras – the wherewithal of the scientific gaze' (Jamie 2012, 148). As she tours the island in the company of a naturalist, an archaeologist and the surveyors, different worlds, human and non-human are revealed to her through their professional gaze. She confesses:

> Being with the surveyors taught me to change my focus. It was like the difference between looking through a window pane and looking at it. Look through the window, and you"d see the sea, wildness, distance, isolation. Look at it, and you saw utility, food security, domestic management. We moved between the Stone Age and the Age of the Satellites. (158)

If the purpose of the expedition is to map out the cultural landscape of the island, exploring the relationship between the environment and human constructions, Jamie is particularly sensitive to the dialogue between the 'scientific gaze' and subjective experience. She learns much from her scientific colleagues and knows that they are central to building an ecological understanding of place, but she wonders how human subjectivity can be situated in the meticulously mapped terrestrial terrain of the 'age of satellites'. The dilemma is best encapsulated in a moment where Jamie has her gaze trained not on island food stores but on the heavens. Watching a lunar eclipse from her Scottish home, she notes: 'Of course I'd seen the Apollo 11 pictures of the blue planet suspended in space, but they made the Earth look homely.' What she was witnessing, 'right now in front of my eyes, was dark, stately and solemn' (124). Jamie nods to the tradition of ocularcentrism in travel writing ('right now in front of my eyes') but also to a dominant ecological construction of earth as the 'blue planet' suspended in all its fragility over the abyssal darkness of space.

One of the most common icons of a globalised age is, not surprisingly, the globe itself. From Jamie's references to the Apollo space mission shots, on the one hand, to the sketchy outline of earth on notices encouraging hotel customers to re-use their towels on the other, the images of the planet are everywhere in the contemporary imaginary. Seeing things from a distance is, of course, and as noted in Section 1, as much a matter of subjection as observation. Occupying a superior vantage point from which one can look down on a subject people or a conquered land is a staple of colonial travel narratives. Tim Ingold, adding a further dimension to the question of distance, draws a distinction between perceiving the environment as a 'sphere' and seeing it as a 'globe'. The classic description of the heavens for centuries in the Western world was of the earth as a sphere with lines running from the human observer to the cosmos above. As geocentric cosmology fell into discredit and heliocentric cosmology came into the ascendant, the image of the sphere gave way to that of the globe. If the sphere presupposed a world experienced and engaged with from within, the globe represented a world perceived from without. Thus, in Ingold's words, 'the movement from spherical to global imagery is also one in which "the world", as we are taught it exists, is drawn ever further from the matrix of our lived experience' (Ingold 2000, 211).

In the movement towards the modern, a practical sensory engagement with the world underpinned by the spherical paradigm is supplanted by a regimen of detachment and control. As the images of the globe proliferate – often, ironically, to mobilise ecological awareness – the danger is that these images themselves distort our relationship to our physical and cultural environment. The effect of continually situating humans at a distance is that they are abstracted and subtracted from local attachments and responsibilities. However, it is precisely such an ability that is often construed as a basic requirement for both national and, more recently, global citizenship. It is the capacity to look beyond the immediate interests of the clan or village or ethnic grouping which creates the conditions for broader definitions of belonging, at a national or indeed global level. But Szersynski and Urry ask the following questions: 'Is this abstraction from the local and particular fully compatible with dwelling in a locality? Could it be that the development of a more cosmopolitan, citizenly perception of place is at the expense of other modes of appreciating and caring for local environments and contexts?' (Szersynski and Urry 2006, 123).

Watching the night sky from her Scottish home, Kathleen Jamie is sensitive to these conflicting loyalties. She acknowledges that 'she could appreciate the earth as an astronaut would, as a heavenly body' but that '[m]ostly if I think of it at all, it's as an indigene, a participant in its daily melee' (Jamie 2012, 124). The tension is explicit between the global visual capture of planetary vulnerability and the irreducibly situated perspective of the 'indigene'. On the other side of the world, walking alone across central Mongolia, Sarah Marquis is grateful that, thanks to her GPS tracking device, her friends and family know 'my exact position at any moment' (Marquis 2016, 75). The Age of the Satellites is a guarantor of personal safety and targeted rescue. She describes her entry into small villages in Mongolia and the routines she goes through to satisfy basic needs (food, water, shopping). Marquis observes: 'Nothing exceptional in these basic needs. Except that, beneath the Mongolian sky, each step of this process is a real challenge. A bit like an adventure within an adventure' (71–2). The satellite device is all about her traceability, but her account is in thrall to her positionality as a white, middle-class, female European travelling on foot through Central Asia. The scientific gaze can locate, but not explain, her. The 'daily melee' of travel with its reminder of basic, human environmental dependency – food, water, shelter – means the traveller must enter the world of the 'indigene' and experience the world as sphere not globe.

Walking is, of course, a radical way of affirming that environmental vulnerability, as there are no screens or engines to insulate and indeed move you through the landscape. The embodied subject of the walker is alert to the affordances and constraints of the natural world. The presence of GPS tracking may call into question the notion of 'remoteness' as an absolute condition, but Marquis's account *Wild by Nature* details the repeated physical challenges of crossing Siberia, Mongolia, the Gobi desert, China, Laos, Thailand and Australia. The world resists. The feet in the sphere complicate the technology of the globe.

Christophe Bonneuil and Jean-Baptiste Fressoz signal the political dangers of blue planet sentimentality, the view from afar:

> The image of the Earth seen from space conveys a radically simplistic interpretation of the world. It gives an intoxicating sense of total overview,

global and dominating, rather than a sense of humble belonging.

(Bonneuil and Fressoz 2016, 92)

The vision of external dominance is of a part with the notion of the proper approach to scientific enquiry as the view from nowhere; impersonal, disembodied, distant and abstract (Daston 1992, 597–618). Malcom Ferdinand, from a Caribbean perspective, challenges the false inclusivity of the blue icon:

Saying that the Earth is home to humanity is to reproduce at planetary level the exclusionist fantasy that conceals the different nature of the actors involved and to avoid the essentially human task of getting along with each other: living *together.* (Ferdinand 2019, 140–1 [emphasis in original])

From an environmental perspective the difficulty with an undifferentiated view of humanity is that some humans bear a much greater responsibility for the climate catastrophe than others. Speaking abstractly of 'humans' or the 'planet' does not address the very real difference in carbon footprint, both in the present and historically, distributed unevenly across the planet (Robinson 2019, 1–19). Critics such as Jason Moore have proposed the term 'Capitalocene' in opposition to Anthropocene arguing that the climate crisis is the direct outcome of the regime of capital accumulation that both drove and was intensified by the Industrial Revolution (Moore 2015; Moore 2016). Given the complicity of travel and tourism in the commodification of nature and the structural imperatives of capitalist development that feed emissions growth, waste and biodiversity loss (Fletcher 2019, 522–35), the generic reach of the 'anthropos' in Anthropocene is deemed to lack explicitness, cloaking direct economic responsibility for dire environmental outcomes.

The human is not a universal, undifferentiated agent but a person defined by categories of race, gender and class and geographical situation that often have a profound bearing on their ecological wellbeing. At one level, it is possible to imagine how the notion of 'globetrotting' and the objectification of the natural world by scientist travellers (Smethurst 2013) point to a particular complicity of travel writers in the construction of an irenic view of an earthly home. At another level, however, we can point to the dogged dissent of writers who see for themselves trails of responsibility and unequal outcomes in environmental devastation.

Paolo Rumiz, travelling along the eastern border of the European Union, is repeatedly witness to the plurality of actors who determine the livelihoods and the environments of the people he encounters. As he travels down from the far north of Europe, Rumiz comments on the evidence of human depredation in the landscape and notes: 'Nature is offended more here, precisely where it is most vulnerable, than it is in any other place on the planet' (Rumiz 2015, 50–1). In

Monchegorsk, near the city of Murmansk, he enters a zone of intense extra-ctivism where cobalt, nickel and copper are mined by thousands of workers. The taxi driver who takes him there is surprised that he wants to spend half a day there because he claims there is nothing to see. Rumiz disagrees:

> But there is a lot to see. At my feet is something new and unprecedented: nature that is sweet and meek, defenseless and violated without mercy, punctuated with mines like pus-filled pimples on an adolescent's face. (59)

For the Italian travel writer, the Kola Peninsula, inside the Arctic Circle, is both heaven and hell: 'There are few places where Earth's suffering is more legible' (60). The industries that supply metals for electrical and IT devices all over the planet are located in 'sacrifice zones'. These zones, according to Naomi Klein, have a number of features in common:

> They were poor places. Out-of-the-way places. Places where residents lacked political power, usually having to do with some combination of race, lan-guage, and class. And the people who lived in these condemned places knew they had been written off. (Klein 2014, 310)

Making his way through a series of sacrifice zones to Odessa on the Black Sea, Rumiz tracks the destruction of forests, the pollution of rivers, the poisoning of the air, the massacre of animals. However, he makes a point of identifying the agents who have come to wreck these earthly homes – large corporations, corrupt oligarchs, affluent tourists, tech giants feeding off a heedless consump-tion of metal-rich IT devices. Travelling by public transport wherever possible, his is the view from the bus not the spaceship. Everything reminds him that he is somewhere rather than nowhere. Remoteness does not involve getting away from it all but rather brings him to what is at the heart of it all, the unspoken environmental price, paid for by the humans he meets, of the systematic destruction of public goods and relentless privatisation. Speaking to local reindeer breeders on the Kola Peninsula, he is made aware of the destruction of indigenous livelihoods by a savage and anarchic hunting down of animals. In a bleak irony, these animals end up as the totemic symbols of the Christmas carnival of conspicuous consumption.

Post-Anthropocentric Travelling

Hannah Arendt, in her prologue to *The Human Condition* (1958), takes the launch of the Sputnik satellite into space in 1957 as a starting point for her reflections on what it is to be human. This travelling object in the heavens becomes a finger pointing to the human desire 'to escape from imprisonment to the earth' (Arendt 1958, 2). The desire to move, the drive for mobility, becomes a form of terrestrial escape, but as Arendt reminds the reader, the terrestrial condition is inescapable:

> The earth is the very quintessence of the human condition, and the earthly nature, for all we know, may be unique in the universe in providing human beings with a habitat in which they can move and breathe without effort and without artifice. The human artifice of the world separates human existence from all mere animal environment, but life itself is outside the artificial world, and through life man remains related to all living organisms. (2)

The human ability to deploy tools, 'artifice', and to create artificial dwellings, large and small, appears to separate humans from all 'mere animal environment'. A long tradition of human exceptionalism, rooted in Christian and Cartesian notions of spiritual superiority and rational pre-eminence, has comforted this apartheid of artifice (Plumwood 2007). In the age of the Anthropocene, such notions have proved to be delusional as anthropogenic climate change reveals that humans are indeed 'related to all living organisms' and will perish in their absence. What, however, are the larger implications of this relationality and how do they situate travel writing in an altered frame of reference?

The biologist Edward O. Wilson in *The Future of Life* (2002) sees specific, long-range historical thinking as essential to curbing humanity, a 'planetary killer, concerned only with its short-term survival' (202). He claims it is only when humans begin to develop species awareness that they can begin to take the longer view. This is vital not only as an important exercise in critical self-understanding but as a way of securing the future. For Rosi Braidotti, this move towards species awareness is a precondition for the development of a post-anthropocentric identity. Such an identity involves the de-centring of *anthropos*, 'the representative of a hierarchical, hegemonic and generally violent species whose centrality is now challenged by a combination of scientific advances and global economic concerns' (Braidotti 2013, 65).

Out of this vision comes a notion of relationality and ontological equality where one life form is not privileged over another. This post-anthropocentric ethics calls for an end to forms of 'anthropolatry' that consign all other species to dangerous, destructive and ecologically untenable forms of subordination. In Braidotti's view, 'becoming animal' makes manifest the irretrievably embodied, material nature of our existence on a planet shared with innumerable other species that continue to be destroyed in large numbers. Reconceiving the notion of human subjectivity to include the non-human means visualising the subject as 'a transversal entity encompassing the human, our genetic neighbours, the animals and the earth as a whole, and to do so within an understandable language' (Braidotti 2013, 82).

One of those understandable languages is travel writing. The language of travel is not the language of academic critique. In its presentation and enactment of travel encounters between the human and the non-human, the travel narrative can gesture towards an emergent transversal subjectivity. On one occasion, Barry Lopez, travel writer and field biologist, falls asleep in the Arctic tundra and wakes to find himself staring at a ground squirrel, in the distance, crouched behind a limestone slab. He notes the actions of the squirrel and wonders if they relate to the presence of predators such as bears, in which case, Lopez, too, ought to exercise caution. He comments on this moment: 'I lay there knowing that something eerie ties us to the world of animals. Sometimes the animals pull you backward into it. You share hunger and fear with them like salt in the blood' (Lopez 2014, 37). Against the backdrop of his Arctic travels, Lopez writes that '[f]ew things provoke like the presence of wild animals. They pull at us like tidal currents with questions of volition, of ethical involvement, of ancestry' (37).

In *Arctic Dreams*, chapters are devoted to muskoxen, polar bears and narwhals, and Lopez is continually exercised by the desire to understand animal behaviour. This is not, however, an exercise in anthropomorphic rapture. When he wonders what is missing that 'makes me so uncomfortable out walking here in a region of chirping birds, distant caribou, and redoubtable lemmings?', the answer is 'restraint' (38). The evolutionary advantage of what Arendt calls 'human artifice' has made certain humans dangerously and destructively indifferent to their relationship to the non-human. It is the hierarchical, hegemonic and violent species ideology condemned by Braidotti that has Lopez so troubled about the future of *Anthropos*. He worries about the ability of the species to control its own appetites.

For Kathleen Jamie, it is internal travels through the human body, in the pathology laboratory of Ninewells Hospital in Dundee, that reveal our kinship with other animals. Using the prose of landscape description to navigate the microscopic worlds of tumorous organs, she heartily agrees with her pathologist host when he marvels: 'Amazing how much like animals we are' (Jamie 2012, 28). She had earlier attended an environmentalists' conference where speakers argued for humanity's necessary relationship with other species. Here was the proof, in a Dundee lab, travelling not through the Arctic tundra but through a cancerous colon.

The revelation of a wider, more-than-human world, of which she is a constituent part, comes for Sarah Marquis in Northern Australia. She notes a 'transformation' that has been at work on her whole being, as two years of travel on foot bring a fundamental shift in outlook:

Two years have put me in a blur . . . and now the fog suddenly lifts, the edges become clear, the colors seem perfect. My transformation took all these steps, all this time. Today I realize that nature lives within me, I am she, she is part of me. Whoa . . . I spend days digesting this harmonic energy with Mother Nature that's so difficult to describe. (Marquis 2016, 208)

Marquis is experiencing what Val Plumwood calls 'life membership in an ecological community of kindred beings' (Plumwood 2009). Contesting what she regards as a reductive rationalism that 'assumes a mindless, materialist universe open to endless, unrestricted manipulation and appropriation', Plumwood pleads for a new animism. This animism rejects the 'passive machine model' of the natural world and draws attention to 'the self-inventive and self-elaborative capacity of nature . . . the intentionality of the non-human world' (Plumwood 2009). Human/nature dualism has the effect of radically separating reason, mind, consciousness from the 'lower order that comprises the body, the woman, the animal and the pre-human' (Plumwood 2009). An animistic materialism reinvests the non-human world with creativity, agency and intentionality.

It is precisely the taxonomic inheritance of a particular kind of scientist traveller that bothers Barry Lopez when he sets out a rationale for what he is doing in his travel writing. He is appreciative of the care that modern field biology takes in describing animals but, echoing the sentiments of the poet Pablo Neruda, suggests it is also 'a task of literature to take animals regularly from the shelves where we have stored them, like charms or the most intricate of watches, and to bring them to life' (Lopez 2014, 129). Part of that task is respecting animal alterity and agency. Lopez acknowledges the prejudice that posits that 'animals are instinctual' and which is 'suspicious of motive and invention among them' (63). Bolstered by his own observations of the polar bear in the Arctic and drawing on the witness accounts of polar bear biologists, he writes of 'the bear's seeming ability to analyze an unfamiliar situation and attempt a practical solution', 'its ability to learn quickly when confronted with something new' and 'the novel approaches bears take to commonplace situations' (103). The more he looks, the more he observes Plumwood's 'self-inventive and self-elaborative capacity of nature'.

Graham Harvey defines philosophical animism as a recognition that 'the world is full of persons, only some of whom are human, and that life is always lived in relationship with others' (Harvey 2006, xi). He points to a crucial dimension to the engagement of contemporary travel writing with the environment, relationality. What is being redrafted is a sense of the transversal self where the world is populated with both human and non-human persons. The question becomes: when we move away from the hyper-separation of nature/

human dualism and the hubris of human exceptionalism, how do human travellers, mindful of their own composite identities, resituate themselves?

On the island of Rona, Kathleen Jamie acknowledges the new humility that is, in part, born out of ecological vulnerability when she comments: 'I say we had the island to ourselves, but of course that's nonsense' (Jamie 2012, 194). She notes the presence of 'seals, and thousands of puffins, and colonies of terns on the low rocks' (194). When Jamie imagines whales that she sees off Rona enjoying the smell of the land she reminds herself that Cetaceans do not have a sense of smell like dogs: '[t]hey may have been only twenty yards away but they inhabited a different sensory world – I'd just made that bit up out of my own humanness' (202). Jamie's self-correction echoes a familiar unease around human projection, the long shadow of anthropomorphic paternalism darkening non-human encounters. Val Plumwood is critical, however, of the too ready accusation of anthropomorphism when there is engagement with the more-than-human, claiming that one of the more recent roles of the concept is that 'of policeman for reductive materialism, enforcing polarised and segregated vocabularies for humans and non-humans' (Plumwood 2009).

Taking up Plumwood's critique of the abuses of anthropomorphism, Deborah Bird Rose argues that the former's philosophical animism entails a notion of interspecies communication:

> She is not defining communication in strictly human terms; there is no suggestion that other creatures sit around debating philosophy, but she is asserting that as other creatures live their lives, so they communicate aspects of themselves. Amidst all this communication, one finds one's self encountering expressiveness and mindfulness within the world of life. And amidst all this mindfulness, there arises a dialogical concept of self for both humans and others. (Rose 2013, 98)

The point of challenging the myth of the non-human world's mindlessness is not then to mindlessly project human desires onto that world but to open oneself up to others as communicative beings. If culture is understood as a specific way of being in the world, then it follows that 'nonhuman beings have, and live by, culture' (100). As Jamie demonstrates with gannets, Lopez with muskoxen and Marquis with ants, other beings are distinguished by particular forms of action. In other words, according to Rose: '[t]hey have their own foods, foraging methods, forms of sociality and seasonality; they have their own languages and their own ceremonies' (100). Culture is not something that is given but something that is expressed in the way one lives and the way knowledge arises out of and responds to particular settings. From the environmental standpoint of this new animism, any form of travel involves moving through 'an entangled matrix of multispecies situatedness' (100). The world is multicultural all the way through.

Time

When humans shift from being biological agents (who work within nature) to geological agents (who shape nature) then the historical frame for human actions changes. The Anthropocene implies momentous changes for the planet, as the result of human activities, so the full impact of those changes can only be understood using the deeply extended geological scale of deep time (Chakrabarty 2009, 197–222).

Travelling in the age of the Anthropocene means standing outside the conventional timescales of human history to embrace a deeper sense of time, not as geological speculation or antiquarian curiosity, but as an urgent task for the present. In *Underland: A Deep Time Journey*, exploring subterranean places on the planet, Robert Macfarlane notes the shift in perspective that follows from the shift in timescale:

> When viewed in deep time, things come alive that seemed inert. New responsibilities declare themselves. A conviviality of being leaps to mind and eye. The World becomes eerily various and vibrant again. Ice breathes. Rock has tides. Mountains ebb and flow. Stone pulses. We live on a restless Earth. (Macfarlane 2019, 15–16)

What Macfarlane reveals on his travels, however, is that infra-human not supra-human vision is needed to detect this restlessness. Travelling down into the limestone landscapes of Somerset, Macfarlane has a sense of stone 'like a liquid briefly paused in its flow' (37), the limestone not inert and obdurate but dynamic and changing. In Epping Forest in London, where he explores the communicative potential of fungi in establishing the 'wood wide web', a network of interspecies communication in the forest, Macfarlane claims that 'living wood seems to *flow* given time' (92 [emphasis in original]).

Observing the interaction between trees and fungi in the forest means that trees become less the symbol of rooted stability and more the nodes in an incessant flow of materials, nutrients and messages. At one point in his forest journey, Macfarlane notes: 'I glance down, try to trance the soil into transparency such that I can see its hidden infrastructure: millions of fungal skeins between tapering tree roots, their prolific liaisons creating a gossamer web at least as intricate as the cables and fibres that hang beneath our cities' (101). This sense of vital materiality, of a profoundly animate world presenting itself to the traveller, takes on a darker meaning in Greenland where Macfarlane witnesses the catastrophic reality of global ice-melt:

> We are now experiencing ice as a newly lively substance. For centuries, the
> polar regions were conventionally imagined as inert: the 'frozen wastes' of
> the north and south. Now, in the context of a warming planet, ice has become
> active again in our imaginations and landscapes. (379)

Ice, for Macfarlane, has always been an active substance. Now, its readily
observable changes where the 'fate of ice will shape planetary futures' (379)
add political drama to geological agency. Throughout his work, Macfarlane
references indigenous understandings of the world, especially their animist
conceptions of the landscape as populated by a variety of sentient beings.
However, the purpose is not to signal an exotic marker of difference or discredit
a putatively pre-rational throwback to earlier forms of thought. It is instead to
explore a more viable notion of transversal subjectivity in the context of
a climate emergency.

   If for many indigenous peoples, 'the jungle or woodland is figured as aware,
conjoined and conversational' (104), then the animism of Macfarlane's subterranean explorations is evidence in travel writing of a movement towards the
new forms of multiculturalism envisaged by Plumwood and Rose. Taking the
travel picturesque and the sublime to task, Macfarlane asserts:

> Nature, too, seems increasingly better understood in fungal terms: not as
> a single, gleaming snow-peak or tumbling river in which we might find
> redemption, nor as a diorama that we deplore or adore from a distance –
> but rather as an assemblage of entanglements of which we are messily part.
> (103)

The spherical perspective aligns with the traveller's experience of a natural
world that is radically altered by extractivist industries, global warming and
waste. A common misunderstanding of animist beliefs is that they involve
a narcissistic projection of the human ego onto the surrounding world. The
anthropologists Deborah Danowski and Eduardo Viveiros de Castro claim, on
the contrary, that it is the 'Moderns' who nourish destructive fantasies of
instrumental mastery:

> According to those we call animists, it is, on the contrary, we, the Moderns,
> who in penetrating into the external space of truth – the dream – only see
> reflections and simulacra of ourselves, instead of opening ourselves to the
> unsettling strangeness of relations with an infinite number of agencies, both
> intelligible and radically other, who are distributed everywhere throughout
> the cosmos. (Danowski and Viveiros de Castro 2014, 285)

The 'dream' is the vision of material wellbeing, the utopia of limitless consumption. By emphasising the distinctness of the 'infinity of agencies',
Amerindian cosmologies highlight the unavoidable negotiation of difference.

For Amerinidian peoples, other animals and entities in the world are treated as 'political entities'. What Westerners know as the environment, Amerindian communities know as 'a society of societies, an international arena, a *cosmopoliteia*' (279).

In Alice Springs, preparing for a trip into the Australian desert, Robyn Davidson becomes aware of 'an assemblage of entanglements of which we are messily part' through her encounters with anti-indigenous racism, misogyny and the long and difficult apprenticeship of living with and training camels. As with the dogs and the crow with which she shares her accommodation, Davidson develops a genuine intimacy with and affection for her non-human companions. Intimacy is not assimilation, however, and she is regularly reminded of the radical alterity of the animals that accompany her on her travels. At one point, she inadvertently finds herself in the way of Dookie, a young bull camel, which is enraged by her presence:

> I yelled maniacally as Dookie pinned me to my side of the gate with his twisted neck and tried to squash me into a cardboard replica. He was leaning into the fence now, trying to smash it so that he could get at me. I could not believe this. This was some nightmare from which I would awake screaming at any moment. My Dookie was a Jekyll and Hyde, a killer, a mad mad mad mad bull. (Davidson 1998, 64)

The affectionate diminutive ('Dookie') gives way to a lucid recognition of irreducible difference. In *Tracks* (1980), preparations for travel and the journey itself school the traveller in a necessary humility, that the more-than-human world has to be negotiated in more-than-human terms.

The recurring difficulty for the travel writer is how to find a language adequate to a post-anthropocentric sensibility. As travellers' tales are primarily a matter of words, how do they accommodate a new animism, a redefined multiculturalism, a move towards a transversal subjectivity? Robert Macfarlane in Greenland confesses: 'Here was a region where matter drove language aside. Ice left language bleached … . Ice would not mean, nor would rock or light, and so this was a weird realm in the old, strong sense of weird – a terrain that could not be communicated in human terms or forms' (Macfarlane 2019, 381). In one sense, this is a recapitulation of familiar Romantic wordlessness in the face of the sublime. In another, however, the dilemma of meaningful relationship – communication – becomes particularly acute in an age where species survival (including humans') depends on humans and non-humans establishing a viable 'ecological community of kindred beings'. Travel writing as a practice that regularly brings the human into contact with the non-human becomes a revealing testing ground for the ethical reach of the post-anthropocentric. The ethics relate not just to what humans do with the non-human, but also to what humans do with or to other humans.

Tourists

On leaving business school in France, Ludovic Hubler decides he would like to see the world. One year out turns into five as he hitchhikes around the globe. Like many travel writers before him, he suffers from the status anxiety brought on by mass tourism. In Morocco, Hubler is torn between aesthetic duty and cultural disquiet:

> Medina quarters, mausoleums, souk markets … Morocco reveals a little more of its magnificence to me each day. If I visit tourist areas, which are an integral part of a country's heritage and which I always strive to explore, I try not to stay too long. There's a reason for this. Relationships between tourists and locals are often artificial and it seems like every interaction must conclude as a transaction. (Hubler 2016, 542).

Hitchhiking itself becomes a mode of travel that distinguishes the young Frenchman from the indiscriminate hordes pounding the well-worn tracks of visitor attractions. Robyn Davidson is ironic about her own longings when she includes among the inhabitants of Alice Springs 'small business operators whose primary function in life is to rip off tourists, who come by the bus-load from America, Japan and urban Australia, expecting high adventure in this last romantic outpost and to see the extraordinary desert which surrounds it' (Davidson 1998, 7–8). Even though Davidson's arduous expedition is in no way comparable to the pitstop sightseeing of bus tourists, she knows that tourists and travellers are forever caught up in a tussle for cultural capital, nervously circling the boundary markers of distinction.

As we saw in the last section, travel writers have long deplored the onslaught, real or imagined, of mass tourism. The note of patrician disdain in Paul Fussell's obituary on travel writing in 1980 (ironically, on the eve of a spectacular revival in the fortunes of the genre) is familiar: 'Because travel is hardly possible anymore, an inquiry into the nature of travel and travel writing between the wars will resemble a threnody, and I'm afraid that a consideration of the tourism that apes it will be like a satire' (Fussell 1980, 37). The massification of travel, in his view, meant the minorisation of the genre. The tyranny of what John Urry termed the 'romantic gaze' – travel as solitary, exclusive and high minded – left travel writers endlessly seeking strategies of differentiation so that travel would remain the privilege of the few and tourism the indulgence of the many (Urry and Larsen 2011, 19).

In the age of the Anthropocene, travel in general and, more specifically, tourism come under scrutiny. The critique is not on the grounds of cultural philistinism but of ecological devastation. When the United Nations proclaimed 2017 to be the International Year of Sustainable Tourism for Development, the prophylactic adjective and the coupling of tourism with development indicated a growing malaise about tourism impacts. Anita Pleumarom from Tourism Concern and Chee Yoke Ling from Third World Network voiced a common complaint when they argued that '[l]ike no other industry, tourism promotes – and glamorizes – a hyper-mobile and hyper-consumeristic lifestyle, rendering sustainability elusive' (Pleumarom and Ling 2017). The litany of negatives matched to tourism was comprehensive and damning: 'gross inequalities, human rights violations, cultural erosion, environmental degradation and climate instability'. The alternatives such as 'green' or 'eco'-tourism were scarcely better as they usually involved long-haul flights, driving climate change, and typically led to the penetration of 'fragile ecosystems and Indigenous Peoples' ancestral lands, triggering both biodiversity loss and cultural loss' (Pleumarom and Ling 2017).

Between 1990 and 2018, world tourist numbers rose from 165 million to 1.4 billion, an increase of more than 750 per cent (Roser 2020), with the predictable environmental consequences of overcrowding, pollution and increased carbon emissions. The globalisation of the world's economies, the deregulation of international air travel, and the end of the Cold War in Europe and Asia (opening up a third of the planet to international tourism) were important factors in this exponential growth in tourist numbers. A study by Yale University revealed that the average cruise ship alone produces around 21,000 gallons of human sewage, one ton of solid waste, 170,000 gallons of waste water, and 8,500 plastic bottles every day (Becker 2013). The long tail of tourism's consequence is outlined by Robyn Davidson. She describes efforts by municipal authorities to remove Aborigines from an encampment on the banks of the River Todd in Alice Springs. The city elders had been 'trying to extend the leases of the properties bordering the river out onto the river-bed itself – a tidy way of getting rid of the camps and making things clean and nice for the tourists, who, after all, spent considerable money buying fake Aboriginal artefacts from the shops' (Davidson 1998).

Paolo Rumiz, for his part, bemoans the privatisation of natural resources for tourism enterprises in Russia, which occurs with the assistance of corrupt local authorities. Comparing the spread of tourism in northern Russia to a toxic weedkiller, he cites the ceding of fishing rights for twenty years on local waterways on the Kola Peninsula to an English company that 'organizes luxury camping tours for salmon fishing' (Rumiz 2015, 67). In each example, local, indigenous populations, whose contribution to climate change has been negligible, are dispossessed to benefit carbon-hungry frequent travellers from affluent urban centres. Humanity may be a 'planetary killer', in Edward O. Wilson's words, but, as tourism shows, humans differ radically in their capacity to destroy. The dark side of mass travel has not gone unnoticed. Initiatives abound to promote a notion of 'ethical tourism'. Luda Berdynk defines an 'ethical tourist' as 'someone who is aware of the consequences and privileges of their actions as a "visitor" on the local environment, whether that includes the local environment, physical environment, or wildlife'. She claims that 'there's somewhat of an unofficial motto amongst ethical tourists: 'Take nothing but pictures, leave nothing but footprints, kill nothing but time'" (Berdynk 2019).

As many examples in this section bear out, travel writers have not been slow to point to the responsibility of particular humans or groups of humans in the ongoing environmental destruction of the planet. The writers both anticipate and articulate the ideology of an ethical tourism. The question remains, however, as to whether travel writing can lay claim to the ecological innocence of its environmental sensitivity. Detailed evocations of the threatened beauty of fragile ecosystems can become one more reason to visit them. In a world of instant commodification (environmental) rapture can turn too readily to (market) capture. Just as the solitary experience of the sublime in the Romantic imagination of the eighteenth century led to mass investment in scenic tourism in the nineteenth century and beyond, how does travel writing avoid becoming complicit in the very forces of environmental destruction that many of its practitioners so actively deplore?

Standing on a beach in Norway, Robert Macfarlane gives voice to an unease that is widespread but that has a particular resonance for a genre dedicated to the revelations of movement:

> Each of us is implicated in the effects of the epoch, each of us an author of its making and its legacies. In the Anthropocene we cannot easily keep nature at a distance, holding it at arm's length for adoration or inspection. Nature is no longer only a remote peak shining in the sun, or a raptor hunting over birchwoods – it is also tidelines thickened with drift plastic, or methane clathrates decomposing over millions of square miles of warming permafrost. This new nature entangles us in ways we are only beginning to comprehend.
> (Macfarlane 2019, 321)

Travel writing has brought readers, as future tourists, to the remote peak and the raptor hunting over birchwoods. Yet, it has also made them aware, of '[s]o much plastic tat' that Kathleen Jamie observes in a gannetry in Scotland (Jamie 2012, 78). Readers now know warming permafrost is fast turning Barry Lopez's arctic dream to a nightmare. Even if the collective 'us' is a dangerous pronoun in an era of sharply differentiated responsibility for climate chaos, Macfarlane's disquiet is especially pronounced in an era when the travel that underpins the writing is itself a significant contributor to environmental collapse.

Subjects/Objects

One feature of climate chaos is that familiar distinctions themselves become chaotic. Subjects are no longer sure about their subjectivity and objects no longer know their place. Travel writing, which in the modern age has been dominated by the overweening emphasis on the individual subject of experience, is now faced with the revolt of objects. Elisabeth Povinelli has coined the term 'geo-ontology' to speak about the worldview of many indigenous groups in Australia that do not establish rigid conceptual and hierarchical distinctions between human subjects and non-human objects (Coleman and Yusoff 2014). Treating rock formations as inert, inanimate matter does not make sense from their geo-ontological perspective where the world in all its variousness is an active part of an animate cosmos. In *Vibrant Matter: A Political Ecology of Things*, the political theorist Jane Bennett argues for a 'vital materiality' that runs through and across bodies, both human and non-human. She claims that the 'quarantines of matter and life encourage us to ignore the vitality *of* matter and the lively powers of material formation' (Bennett 2010, vii [emphasis in original]).

Acknowledging this 'vital materiality' is not simply a matter of giving 'things' their due. In terms of a tradition of first-person narrative that has dominated travel accounts in late modernity, the inherent strangeness of the other-than-human undermines any sense of a complacent subjectivity that might attend the primacy of the first person. Timothy Morton, drawing on the object-oriented ontology of Graham Harman (2018), sees a clear relationship between subject hubris and climate horror:

> Correlationism, the idea that the world isn't real until some correlator (usually tied to a human being in some way) has 'realized' it, can produce the fantasy that reality is a blank slate waiting for (human) projections to fill it in, like a movie screen waiting for a movie to be shown on it. The idea that the world is a blank canvas waiting for the correlator to paint on it is rather obviously ecologically violent: the world is not a blank screen, it's a coral reef, it's a high-altitude Alpine ecosystem, it's a humpback whale. (Morton 2018, 206)

A common version of this outlook is a form of cultural constructivism that argues that things are only when we (humans) say they are. When non-human things (viruses, floodwaters, plastic, climate) intervene in increasingly vivid and catastrophic ways in human lives (some, of course, more affected than others), what is revealed are the cruel limits to subjective idealism. There is the clear sense that no 'one access mode can exhaust all the qualities and characteristics of a thing' (21).

Writing about the Narwhal, Barry Lopez talks about the 'need for a respectful attitude towards a mystery we can do no better than name "Narwhal"' (Lopez 2014, 140). Arguably, in the age of the Anthropocene, this respectful attitude needs to be extended to the entire material universe. Travel writers as (human) subjects are narrating a world where the (non-human) objects are fighting back. For a genre deeply bound up with the activities and ruminations of a (frequently white, male, middle-class) subject, where subjectivity is the guarantor of authenticity (I was there; this is what happened), how does the more-than-human world find a voice? How are the limits to knowingness and default correlationism to be acknowledged? If humans cannot transcend their species' condition (they remain irreducibly and biologically human), is there a role for travel writing in an age of anthropogenic climate change?

Being Ecological

Ludovic Hubler hints at one answer to these questions when he speaks of what he had learned from five years hitchhiking around the world: 'I have been changed by my world tour. It has enabled me to rekindle my curiosity, opened up my mind, and undermined my certitudes and preconceptions' (Hubler 2016, 320). Travelling challenged his prejudices and changed his outlook, particularly around ecological questions, the result of witnessing the consequences of deforestation in Honduras, Brazil and Indochina and melting glaciers in the Antarctica (553). Central to his experiences of elsewhere, however, was joy. The variousness of the world was a source of renewed happiness throughout his journey. In this credo, repeatedly recited by the other writers discussed in this section, lies an important antidote to the toxic tone of much environmental commentary.

Timothy Morton, in *Being Ecological*, warns the reader from the outset that their book is 'largely free of facts' (Morton 2018, 4). They claim the main ecological information delivery mode in the media is what they dub '*an information dump*' (9 [emphasis in original]). One terrifying statistic after another is aligned in a shooting gallery of righteous fury. Morton speculates that the readers may be informed but not necessarily *trans*formed. If they were, there would be no climate crisis. The difficulty, in his view, is to '*live* ecological knowledge' because it 'seems to be not enough just to know stuff' (11 [emphasis in original]). Muddling through an information dump of doomsday data may cause the concerned citizen to curl up in foetal despair rather than live out ecological information in any meaningful way. For Morton, at present, 'the ways in which we talk to ourselves about ecology are stuck in horror mode: disgust, shame, guilt' (60). Indeed, as we have seen in this section, there is understandably much in contemporary travel writing that expresses the 'horror mode', the relentless detailing of environmental calamities.

There is also, however, a bearing witness to the beauty and unsurpassable variety of the world. Caring is as much about celebration as about condemnation. A typical glimpse into this exhilaration of being in the world is provided by Robyn Davidson when she describes the beginning of her camel trek across the desert:

> All around me was magnificence. Light, power, space and sun. And I was walking into it. I was going to let it make me or break me. A great weight lifted off my back. I felt like dancing and calling to the great spirit. Mountains pulled and pushed, wind roared down chasms. (Davidson 1998, 101)

The magnificence of the surroundings becomes its own argument. Information about environmental uniqueness is conveyed but it is not the numerical accountability of despair. In spite of the almost unavoidable human projection ('I was going to let it make me or break me'), the traveller attests to the value of this immersion in the more-than-human world. In sum, travel writing provides an alternative mode of delivering ecological information. There is a way of communicating the climate crisis that is neither the information dump nor the horror show. These are both present to varying degrees in different travel accounts but it is the capacity for joy and imaginative empathy that releases travel writing into a different space of communicative possibility.

While travel literature is defined by mobility, it is useful to remember that it is still 'literature', a specific form of writing, an aesthetic practice. This specificity takes on a particular importance in the context of environmental disruption. Val Plumwood in her project of 're-animating the world, and remaking ourselves . . . to become multiply enriched but consequently constrained members of an ecological community' envisages a central role for "poetry and literature' (Plumwood 2009). Deborah Bird Rose, drawing on Plumwood's legacy, argues that the search for 'poetic forms of writing' is motivated by the need in the age of the Anthropocene 'to vivify, to leap across imaginative realms, to connect, to empathise, to be addressed and to be brought into gratitude' (Rose 2013, 106). Consciously drawing on the narrative resources of fiction and the expressive possibilities of poetic language, travel writing has the capacity to give real meaning to ecological literacy. Sylvain Tesson, in Tibet on the tracks of the snow leopard, speculates on the conditions of that literacy. Accompanying the photographer Thierry Munier, he spends days and weeks patiently awaiting the appearance of the reclusive animal. He observes that: '[w]hile my friends scrutinised the world through their binoculars, I was looking for an idea, worse still, a clever turn of phrase' (Tesson 2019, 114). Tesson proclaims his indebtedness to the French writer Jules Renard, asserting that Renard 'blessed the beauty of the world with the only thing at his disposal: words' (114). In the course of his Tibetan expedition, Tesson learns that being still is as instructive as moving on:

> I had learned that patience is a supreme virtue, the most elegant and the most neglected. It helped you to love the world before claiming to change it. It invited you to sit before the stage, and enjoy the performance, even if it was the trembling of a leaf. Patience was man bowing down before what is. (161–2)

Patience for Tesson is what allows the painter to paint, the composer to compose and the writer to write. Discretion, stillness and patience allow a world to emerge that is richly populated by the non-human, by the animate worlds of the organic and the material. Quoting from 'A Memorable Fancy' in *The Marriage of Heaven and Hell* by William Blake ('How do you know but ev'ry Bird that cuts the airy way/ Is an immense world of delight, clos'd by your senses five?'), Tesson acknowledges that witnessing is not knowing. He and Munier understood that there was much of the natural world that they encountered but did not understand and 'we were happy with that' (165). There is no sentimentality in the murderous encounters between different species in the Tibetan heights. This is no Disney menagerie of cuddly megafauna. The travel writer is all too aware of the more general ecological catastrophe he deplores in his work, but like his photographer companion, he does not simply want to be another 'witness to disaster' (103). Rendering the beauty of the animals and their environment is their way of mounting a defence against the forces of extinction. If Morton argues that 'ecological politics is about expanding, modifying and developing new forms of *pleasure*, not restraining the meagre pleasures we already experience' (Morton 2018, 210), then the punitive superego of the horror mode must make room for less abrasive, more joyous, ways of remaking.

Part of being ecological is a capacity for connection or reconnection. On a visit to an underground cave noted for its stalagmites and prehistoric art, Kathleen Jamie comments on the fury of interpretation. The stalagmites are metaphorically compared by the guide to human construction ('castle') and community ('family'). Reasons are advanced and speculated on for the motives behind the depiction of animals on the cave walls. Jamie wonders whether the main drivers for human cultural evolution are not, on the one hand, the 'discriminations and resentments … (You, but not you)' and, on the other, 'our ability, born perhaps of thousands of years of watching the transforming play of firelight – to think in simile, in metaphor' (Jamie 2012, 170–1).

Division and connection, 'taxonomies' and 'connective leaps', these are binary building blocks of human reflection. As we noted in Section 1, taxonomic preoccupation was central to forms of engagement in scientific travel writing with the natural world in the seventeenth and eighteenth centuries (see also Bertrand 2019). The poetic ability to wield simile or use metaphor is continuously present in the prose of travel, as Barry Lopez reminds readers when he describes hearing snow geese: 'The single outcries became a rising cheer, as if in a far-off stadium, that rose and fell away' (Lopez 2014, 152). Both the desire to discriminate and the desire to connect are arguably part of an aesthetic impulse which aims to understand in a more complete way.

As Robert Macfarlane puts it, writing about Lopez: 'While writing about landscape often begins in the aesthetic it ends in the ethical' (Macfarlane 2015, 211). Travel literature as an adjunct to being ecologically, a way of living with ecological knowledge, is critically bound up with what Morton has called the 'context explosion' of ecological awareness (Morton 2018, 88). The felled trees Hubler sees in Indonesia, the plastic Jamie comes across in gannets' nests in Scotland, the calving glaciers Macfarlane observes in Greenland, they all have as their contexts a multitude of discrete human actions, predominantly in the Global North, that translate into baleful ecological outcomes.

Travel writing in an age of environmental crisis tracks the multiplying contexts of human acts to show that everything is connected: the plastic rope and the bird's nest, the bedside table and the forest, the boiling kettle and the melting ice. The parts are greater than their sum because there is no way of containing the partial contextual fallout of ecological malpractice just as the parts themselves are not interchangeable to retrieve some lost reductive whole ('God', 'Nature', 'Cosmos'). The species detailed by Lopez, Jamie, Tesson, once gone are gone. Part of travel writing's fractal attentiveness to place is the indefinite exploration of environmental context, the endless connection of parts to other parts, driven by the 'connective leaps' of language. As travel writers have repeatedly reminded us in the modern age, there is nothing natural about the End of Nature. But what happens when the End of Nature means the End of Travel?

3 The End of Travel?

'Travel writers, and travel writing critics, have been proclaiming the end-of-travel for at least a century and a half' (Graulund 2019, 271; see also Graulund 2016, 285–95). Rune Graulund's terse summary of the long lament for lost romance, associated with an infinitely receding age of intrepid exploration, is telling. Developments in transport, communications and the leisure economy mean travel writing can only mourn its subject as a McDisneyfied world remains corralled in the echo chambers of Facebook Likes. As Graulund notes, '[p]aradoxical as it may seem, increased mobility has prompted many travel writers to claim that travel is dying, or perhaps already dead' (273). The familiar threnody, with its suggestion of the jaded palate of exhausted elites and a nostalgia for the vanished proprieties of empire and class, has given way to a more urgent concern around the existential threats posed not *to* travel but *by* travel.

Flight Shame

Manchán Magan, a travel writer and journalist, opened his newspaper column on 25 January 2020 with a dramatic declaration of intent: 'I could never have predicted a year ago that I would be writing this article proclaiming my intention to give up flying abroad on holidays' (Magan 2020, 34). Living on an island on the edge of Europe, deriving his main income from a weekly travel column, he was not making an easy decision but nonetheless declared:

> It had to stop. I'm responsible for coaxing too many people to fly already. Have I the soot of their carbon emissions on my hands? Either way, I cannot continue to promote the further pollution of this planet, poisoning it for future generations just so I can take free holidays and get paid to report on them. (34)

Magan was drawing the logical conclusion from what climate science had been telling him. Since 1990, carbon dioxide emissions from international aviation have increased 83 per cent. One of the special characteristics of aircraft emissions is that most of them are produced at cruising altitudes high in the atmosphere. These high-altitude emissions have a more harmful climate impact as they trigger a series of chemical reactions that increases the net warming effect. The International Panel on Climate Change (IPCC) has estimated that the climate impact of aircraft is two to four times greater than the effect of their carbon dioxide emissions alone (Timperley 2017). Emissions from flying stand to triple by 2050 if demand for air travel continues to grow. As Andrew Murphy, an aviation manager at Transport & Environment, a think tank based in Brussels, has pointed out: 'Euro for euro, hour for hour, flying is the quickest and cheapest way to warm the planet' (Irfan 2019).

If the Swedish term *flygskam* (flight-shaming) were to become part of the vocabulary of the international environmental movement, the Covid-19 pandemic in 2020 would provide a graphic illustration of what the end-of-travel might look like. The combination of lockdowns and quarantine regulations meant that all forms of mobility were affected, but the consequences for air travel were dramatic. Passenger air transport dropped by 90 per cent between April 2019 and April 2020 (OECD 2020, 3). The pandemic was, of course, a reflection of the wider environmental crisis, more symptom than outlier. As the noted historian of epidemics, Frank M. Snowden pointed out, each age gets the pandemic it deserves:

> COVID-19 flared up and spread because it is suited to the society we have made. A world with nearly eight billion people, the majority of whom live in densely crowded cities and all linked by rapid air travel, creates innumerable opportunities for pulmonary viruses. At the same time, demographic increase and frenetic urbanization lead to the invasion and destruction of animal habitat, altering the relationship of humans to the animal world.
>
> (Snowden 2020, ix)

The ecological disruption (zoonotic transmission) that was the necessary context for the pandemic was magnified in its effects on human societies by continuous air travel. The end-of-travel in the age of the Anthropocene is no longer a dystopian fiction but a lived reality. The sense of the end becomes more real than imagined when travel writers imagine the soot of their readers' carbon emissions on their hands and when Taipei International Airport sells tours in which members of the public go through security and clear immigration before taking their seats on flights that never take off (Butler 2020, 8). Travel is now keyed to present, existential threat rather than sepia-tinged disenchantment. It is no longer a question of mass travel making everywhere look the same or of tourism contributing to localised environmental pollution. It is very act of travelling that becomes problematic. The era of global space–time convergence ushered in by mass air travel has made the world not so much a smaller place as an infinitely more dangerous one.

When Mark O'Connell in *Notes from an Apocalypse* decides to embark on his 'perverse pilgrimages', his journeys to places where the end of the world might be glimpsed, he is only too painfully aware of the cruel paradox of his decision:

> You will note that this book about the apocalyptic tenor of our time features a great many interludes of travel to distant places – to Ukraine and California and South Dakota, to the highlands of Scotland and New Zealand – and that I neither walked nor sailed nor took a train to any of these places. And let the record further show that during the time I was traveling for this book, I was also traveling to many other places to talk about my previous book. My footprint is as broad and deep and indelible as my guilt. (O'Connell 2020, 9)

The mode of travel participates in the end of travel, carbon-rich contributions to an ecological apocalypse of the author's own making. The subtitle for

O'Connell's work is 'Personal Journey to the End of the World and Back' and he dutifully journeys to the ends of the earth, tracking places where individuals or groups prepare for a post-apocalyptic world. It might be, however, that the end of travel is not about the end of travel per se but about the end of a certain kind of travelling. In other words, the climate crisis compels writers and readers to think about 'new kinds of travel and, by extension, new ways of articulating and understanding travel' (Edwards and Graulund 2012, 98).

Verticality

Changed circumstances can trigger finer distinctions, and earlier discriminations take on a new relevance. In a previous work, drawing on research by the French travel theorist Jean-Didier Urbain (1998), I distinguish between vertical and horizontal travel. Horizontal travel is the more common understanding of travel, the linear journey from one place to the next, removed in distance and in time (the time it takes to get there). Vertical travel involves remaining in proximity to the point of departure, travelling down into the particulars of a place, either in space (e.g. botanical description) or time (local history, archaeology, etc.) (Cronin 2000, 19). Horizontal travel implies leaving familiar surroundings for a place that is generally situated at some remove from the routine world of the traveller. Vertical travel, by way of contrast, is an exercise in staying close by, not leaving the familiar and travelling interstitially through a world previously assumed to be known.

Alasdair Pettinger notes how 'vertical travel emerged in the wake of more than two decades of rapidly proliferating accounts of highly circumscribed journeys in which the author hardly travels at all, but brings to familiar surroundings a degree of curiosity normally associated with unfamiliar places for the first time' (Pettinger 2019, 797). If the end of the twentieth century and the beginning of the twenty-first century have witnessed a marked increase in attention to vertical travel, this is, in part, shadowed by an ecological and ethical necessity, the need to engage in more sustainable, locally based patterns of production and consumption.

The practices of vertical travel are extremely various. In *Tentative d'épuisement d'un lieu parisien*, the French author Georges Perec engages in exploring what he dubs the 'infra-ordinary' (Perec 1989). He compulsorily lists all the goings-on in and around the Café de la Mairie adjacent to the Saint Sulpice church in Paris (Perec 1982). The aim of Perec's method is to make evident the sheer scale of the infra-ordinary, the encyclopedic density of things literally taking place in our immediate surrounding that generally pass unnoticed. A context for Perec's vertical travel writing is a broader concern in

French progressive thinking with challenging people's alienation from their surroundings, a retrieval of purpose in and power over the everyday world (Sherringham 2006).

The tradition of proximate ethnography that draws on the anthropological tradition of the detailed description of small communities informs accounts where the usual poles of enquiry are reversed. The domestic, not the foreign, becomes the focus of analytic enquiry. Marc Augé treats the Parisian Metro as if it were an unknown and hitherto unexplored ethnographic terrain, familiar worlds rendered other through the professional ethnographer's probing inquisitiveness (Augé 2002). Alain de Botton in *A Week at the Airport: A Heathrow Diary* takes the point of departure for horizontal travel as a point of arrival for vertical travel as he moves through the nested worlds of a major international airport (de Botton 2009).

Xavier de Maistre's *Voyage autour de ma chambre* (1794) started out as a satire on the horizontal travel accounts of the Grand Tour. In his account, de Maistre treats his bedroom in Paris as if it were a vast, uncharted and perilous territory where moving from his bed to a chair has all the adventure of an expedition on the high seas. This form of interstitial travel writing has continued into the modern period with accounts such as François Maspero's *Roissy Express: A Journey through the Paris Suburbs* (1994). Maspero accompanies the photographer Anaïk Frantz on a trip from Roissy airport to the end of the RER B railway line, a trip that normally takes little over an hour. Their journey, however, lasts two months, with stops at each of the stations on the way to central Paris and beyond, revealing whole other worlds normally invisible to the traveller who hurtles through seemingly featureless spaces on the way from the airport to the city. One of the most salient features of Maspero's decelerated Odyssey is coming into contact with migrants speaking a plurality of languages and bringing with them a variety of spoken and unspoken cultures and histories. The interstices, the stops along the way, reveal worlds of infinitely receding fractal complexity.

Alexandra Horowitz travels through her Manhattan neighbourhood over and over again, each time with a different companion – a child, a dog, an urban sociologist, an artist, a physician, a sound designer – all the while schooling herself in attention, walking with people 'who have distinctive, individual, expert ways of seeing all the unattended, perceived ordinary elements I was missing' (Horowitz 2013, 3). Common to all forms of vertical travel are strategies of defamiliarisation. They compel the reader to look afresh, to call into question the taken for granted, to take on board the infinitely receding complexity of the putatively routine or prosaic. They suggest that shrinkage is a matter not of scale but of vision. A narrowing of focus, a reduction in reach can, in fact, lead to an expansion of insight, an unleashing of interpretive and imaginative possibilities often smothered by an overweening emphasis on the benefits of horizontal mobility.

The emergence of the vertical paradigm in travel writing aligns the practice with the conceptual and cultural revolution called for by the climate emergency. Paul Virilio in *The Futurism of the Instant* argues that, if the twentieth century witnessed the revolution of externalisation, the twenty-first century would demand the revolution of internalisation. Chronicling changes in contemporary experiences of time and space, he notes 'the importance now attached by firms to the EXTERNALISATION of their production – including research and development – at the expense of their former specific local base. So, for several years now, the *external* has become more important everywhere than the *internal* and geophysical history is turned inside out like a glove!' (Virilio 2010, 19 [emphasis in original]).

Externalisation has, of course, been a core feature of the global economic system in late modernity and led to exponential increases in the consumption of fossil fuels (Klein 2019, 70–103). In a sense, forms of externalisation have been in evidence ever since David Ricardo formulated his theory of comparative advantage. Industrialised nations import agricultural produce from nations that enjoy the comparative advantage of still possessing fertile land for food production. These nations, in turn, buy manufactured goods with earnings from the sale of foodstuffs and begin their own process of industrialisation. Travel writers in this Element's previous sections have borne witness, in different ways, to the consequences of the revolution of externalisation for different places and peoples.

The limits to externalisation are evident in the human impact on terrestrial ecosystems, as detailed by a report from the Institute for Public Policy Research in the United Kingdom. More than 75 per cent of the earth's land is substantially degraded: topsoil is now being lost ten to forty times more quickly than it is being replenished by natural processes; 30 per cent of the world's arable land since the mid-twentieth century has become unproductive due to erosion; and 95 per cent of the earth's land areas could become degraded by 2050 (Laybourn-Langton, Rankin and Baxter 2019, 6–7). The authors of *This is a Crisis* are explicit about the repercussions:

Human-induced environmental change is occurring at an

> unprecedented scale and pace and the window of opportunity to avoid catastrophic outcomes in societies around the world is rapidly closing. These outcomes include economic instability, large-scale involuntary migration, conflict, famine and the potential collapse of social and economic systems. The historical disregard of environmental considerations in most

areas of policy has been a catastrophic mistake.

(Laybourn-Langton, Rankin and Baxter 2019, 6)

The revolution of externalisation, which both facilitated and was facilitated by extensive horizontal travel in the modern era, has run its course. The coming revolution is the revolution of internalisation. Transport, industry, architecture, agriculture, energy and finance will have to radically reverse the compulsive externalisation of the globalised market economy and move to practices of self-reliance and resilience for any transition to a low-carbon economy to be feasible. It is in this context that vertical travel writing practices need to be situated, as one way of reimagining travel and writing in the age of the Anthropocene. In pointing up the conventions vertical travel writing seeks to subvert – 'horizontal expansiveness; a yearning for wilderness free of traces of humanity; solipsism redolent of much Romantic travel' (Forsdick 2020, 101) – Charles Forsdick could equally be describing the hankering after a culture of infinite growth, a fantasy of unlimited horizontal externality.

The pleasures of verticality are not always seen, however, as an unalloyed good. E. M. Forster, writing in 1915, complained that England 'felt tighter and tinier and shinier than ever – a very precious little party, I don't doubt, but most insistently an island, and there are times when one longs to sprawl on continents, as formerly' (cited in Fussell 1980, 10). Even allowing for the imperial undertow of the desire to 'sprawl on continents', the sentiment is recognisable. There is the anxiety of shrinkage, the embattled parochialism, the defensive local allegiance of the particular that leaves no place for the broader sympathies of journeying to other peoples and places. Horizontal travel, at its most Utopian, can suggest a universal love for all peoples and all species, a kind of radical externalisation of sentiment that envelops the planet in an outward burst of fellow feeling. But, are internal repudiation and external celebration the only grounds for intelligent sympathy or due care?

Val Plumwood has expressed a useful scepticism with respect to the viability of sympathies which are too indiscriminate in their focus, the pratfalls of 'universal' love:

> [T]his 'transpersonal' identification is so indiscriminate and intent on denying particular meanings, it cannot allow for the deep and highly particularistic attachment to place that has motivated both the passion of many modern conservationists and the love of many indigenous peoples for their land.
>
> (Plumwood 1994, 152)

Plumwood argues that, in fact, it is internalisation not externalisation that becomes the effective basis for meaningful engagement with struggles and issues elsewhere:

> Care and responsibility for particular animals, trees, and rivers that are known well, loved and appropriately connected to the self are an important basis for acquiring a wider, more generalized concern. (145–6)

The dual impulse of care and responsibility drives the 'deep mapping' movement in vertical travel where writer/cartographers like Tim Robinson and William Least Heat-Moon track in forensic detail their journeys through reduced spaces – offshore islands, disregarded badlands – but continuously point up their connections to elsewhere (Pettinger 2019, 800; Roorda 2001, 259–72). It is, in fact, the local connection, the ready identification of a particular animal, tree, river, predatory oil company or abusive state practice in a local setting that makes possible the ethical imagining of the importance of species preservation or social justice in other proximate, micro-sites. The movement inwards is an opening up, not a shutting down or out. As Alastair McIntosh has observed: 'I must start where I stand. As children, we used to be told that if you dug a really deep hole, you'd come out in Australia. I think in some ways this is very true. If any of us dig deep enough where we stand, we will find ourselves connected to all parts of the world' (McIntosh 2002, 7). In this sense, internalisation becomes a highly effective form of mobilisation in starting from concrete, near-to-hand examples to address issues that have a resonance beyond a specific locale. The two practices are, of course, not mutually exclusive and, as we have amply observed in previous sections, concrete near-to-hand examples of environmental peril punctuate horizontal accounts as the travel writers dwell, however temporarily, in particular places. The question in the age of anthropogenic climate change is the relative importance of vertical and horizontal practices in travel writing projects and how they are to be reconciled with the carbon cost of displacement.

Virtual Virtues

One move in the context of a climate emergency is not to move at all. In 2013, writing about the future of travel writing in the twenty-first century, Tim Youngs opened a section on 'Cybertravel' with the claim that '[t]ravel writing, like all literature, responds to new technologies' (Youngs 2013, 178). One function of the Internet can be to provide an outlet for the publication of accounts of actual travel experiences as described by Youngs. Another is to offer a forum for the delivery of virtual travel experiences. During the Covid-19 pandemic, when 90 per cent of the world's population were under travel restrictions, virtual travel went viral (Garry 2020;McClanahan and Karim 2020). Travel correspondents with no possibility of movement filed reports on what was out there on the electronic frontier. The sightseeing of the tourist gave way to the site seeing of the cybertraveller.

In April 2020, Paige McClanahan and Debra Karim – who had, three months earlier, published a list of fifty-two places to visit that year – told readers of *The New York Times* that 'given our stay-at-home circumstances, we'd like to invite you on a series of virtual journeys: You can wander into the belly of an Egyptian pyramid, explore the house where Mozart was born, or fly over the rocky peaks of Glacier National Park' (McClanahan and Karim 2020). When *The Irish Times* asked the question 'what do travel writers do when they can't leave home?', one such writer described watching hours of in-cab railway videos, the ten-hour Trondheim to Bodø route produced by the Norwegian state broadcaster NRK, and the full 9,000 km journey of the Transsiberian railway, produced jointly by Russian Railways and Google (Ganatra et al. 2020, 25). Angela Chan, writing for *National Geographic* on Earth Day 2020, argued that virtual travel could be virtuous travel. She claimed that people who might usually have celebrated the day by going outdoors, 'might need to rely on virtual tours instead' and that it was a 'fitting opportunity to experience a technology that some experts have advanced as an eco-friendly solution to the problem of overtourism' (Chan 2020). Platforms such as Google Earth VR facilitate these forms of virtual travel, and headsets such as Oculus Rift allow for 360°-views of sites in the world's leading travel destinations (Garry 2020). If George Monbiot argues that 'long-distance-travel, high speed and the curtailment of climate change are not compatible' (Montbiot 2006, 188) then the screen might literally be a saver. No need for all the airmiles if a click can connect. Does this mean in terms of the environmental impact of travel that the only virtue lies in the virtual? Is travel writing still necessary when 'virtual reality might bring faraway places closer and in so doing encourage travelers to embrace sustainable practices' (Chan 2020)?

We might begin by pointing out that there is nothing virtual about the ecological impact of the virtual. It is damagingly real. Smartphones, servers and laptops all contain metals that are difficult to extract and difficult, if not impossible, to recycle. The exponential increase in the number of IT devices, the privatisation of usage, the ongoing growth in data centres that generate so much heat that it is necessary to systematically cool them down, all contribute to the consumption of energy resources whose exploitation is a major contributing factor to climate change (de Decker 2015). The emissions are no less real for being less visible.

Another observation might be that travel writing is, by definition, virtual travel. No reader has ever been literally transported by a book. Travelling to a different place is wholly the work of the reader's imagination interacting with the narrative strategies of the writer. Alison Byerly writes about how the increasing Victorian interest in 'staying at home and fantasizing about travel'

(Byerly 2012, 2) is facilitated by 'virtual travel' as experienced through 360° panoramas, foldout river maps, railway guides and travel accounts. The armchair traveller knows what it is to have 'faraway places' brought closer without feeling that they have left a carbon footprint beyond their front door (see Stiegler 2013).

Jamie Ball's advice to newspaper readers no longer able to physically travel during the Covid-19 pandemic was that they should immerse themselves in 'the greats of travel literature over the last century'. The ecological challenge of travel restrictions intimated the need for a rediscovery of 'our more curious, bookish ancestors' who 'read with wonder, awe, dread and inspiration of locations they had no means of ever being able to visit, so they travelled in their mind instead' (Ganatra et al. 2020, 26). The mind travelling of the travel narrative is, however, a virtual tour of a particular kind. In exploring the concept of 'virtual travel', Margaret Topping contends that the 'virtual may facilitate an understanding of the world in a unified way, but there must also be a gap between direct experience and mediated experience; otherwise the risk is that the seamless multisensory experiences such technologies facilitate conceals their own constructedness' (Topping 2019, 806).

The effort required of the reader to reconstruct sights, sounds, sensations, whole worlds, based on words on a page, is a kind of interpretive safeguard. It is precisely the distance between the written symbols and the realities evoked, often seen as a constitutive weakness of the genre ('no description can do justice to the beauty of the scenery between Amalfi and Castellammare' [Blessington 1839, 353]), that opens up spaces of multiple meanings, multiple understandings. Which is not to argue, of course, that travel writing does not have its forms of 'constructedness', more or less concealed from the reader. A central argument of this Element is that the natural world has been articulated by travel writers, in different periods, in ways that have profoundly shaped readers' attitudes and responses to the environment. However, the phenomenological immediacy of immersion in a virtual environment makes mediation problematic. Imaginative indiscipline and the powers of association that come with 'horizontal movement through the text' (Topping 2019, 807) are not readily part of the experience.

Angela Chan, for her part, acknowledges that, on 'a fundamental level, virtual travel is constructed and fed to us; we see a world only to the extent that someone was able to film and engineer it' and she goes on to cite a virtual reality theorist Erick Ramirez who claims that virtual travel is 'the most authoritarian of guided tours' (Chan 2020). The active, hermeneutic labour of reading means that meanings are never overdetermined, words and texts are received differently at different moments, in different ways. The 'preservation of uncertainty and physical and psychological discomfort' (Topping 2019, 805) is central to the construction of the sentimental traveller from Laurence Sterne onwards. When Sterne's narrator in *A Sentimental Journey through France and Italy* insists that 'there is no regular reasoning upon the ebbs and flows of our humours; they may depend upon the same causes, for aught I know, which influence the tides themselves' (Sterne 1892, 559), he is entering into a pact with the readers of his travel account. This is what they should expect: uncertainty and psychological, if not also physical, discomfort. But it is precisely 'physical discomfort' and the place of physicality itself in the world of virtual travel that raise important questions around the engagement of travel writing with the natural environment.

Wild By Nature

The philosopher Charles Taylor speaks of the specific boundedness and vulnerability of human inquiry. He contrasts the picture of the human thinking agent as disengaged, disincarnate, speaking from nowhere in particular, with twentieth-century attempts to rethink the nature of agency. Taylor sees both Heidegger and Wittgenstein as struggling in different ways 'to recover an understanding of the agent as engaged, as embedded in a culture, a form of life, a "world of involvements", ultimately to understand the agent as embodied' (Taylor 1995, 61–2). As feminist scholars have pointed out, the rational, disincarnate agent is almost invariably male (Plumwood 1993). Human/nature dualism typically separates the thinking agent from what Val Plumwood has identified as the 'lower order that comprises the body, the woman, the animal and the pre-human' (Plumwood 2007). A graphic illustration of the reality of that embodied self are the restrictions women face in their movements because of their bodies, sexualised and variously controlled by the male gaze.

In her 1893 essay entitled 'The Bondage of Women' following a brief historical survey of the condition of women, Jane Wilde concluded: 'We have now traced the history of women from Paradise to the nineteenth century, and have heard nothing through the long roll of ages but the clank of their fetters' (Wilde 1893, 13). Commenting on women's mobility more than a century later, Rebecca Solnit finds little to disagree with in Wilde's assessment: 'Travel, whether local or global, has remained a largely masculine prerogative ... with women often the destination, the prize, or keepers of the hearth' (Solnit 2014, 235). If walking is a primary experience of the incarnate self – of the body in motion, in contact with the world around it, free from the disincarnate realities of virtual technologies – then experience is itself deeply gendered. Walking in certain places, at certain times of the day or night, in urban, suburban or rural spaces can become problematic, if not downright dangerous, for women. Noo Saro-Wiwa speaks of her younger self: 'In my student days, my plans and ambitions were unfettered by any sense of limitation. I felt able to do anything, travel anywhere, pursue any line of work' (Saro-Wiwa 2013, 91). Her subsequent experiences, and travels through Nigeria, demonstrate how sharply both movements and ambitions can be curtailed. When a nineteen-year old Sylvia Plath confesses that 'I want to be able to sleep in an open field, to travel west, to walk freely at night' (cited in Solnit 2014, 233), the impossibility of the wish clearly shows that, although the natural world has often been construed as a realm of liberty for some, the freedom to roam in that world is heavily determined by gender.

One of the crueller paradoxes of the forms of social control around women's movement is that their identification with 'nature' is precisely what has been used to justify their exclusion from the Great Outdoors. The historical control of female sexuality has involved 'controlling and defining female sexuality often viewed as chaotic, threatening and subversive – a sort of wild nature to be subdued by masculine culture' (236). Controlling or 'improving' wild nature is also a project of controlling or improving 'wild' women or women who, literally, do not know their place. In giving the title *Wild by Nature* to her three-year trek across Asia and Australia, Sarah Marquis is doubling back on the stereotype, taking it as an invitation to break the rules rather than respecting the conventions. In dedicating her travel account: 'To all the women throughout the world who are still fighting for their freedom', she is aligning the body of her text with the bodies of women who have been told from the time of Xenophon onwards that '[y]our business will be to stay indoors' (cited in Solnit 2014, 236).

In a sombre echo of extractivist approaches to the natural world and mass species destruction, Rebecca Solnit uses the metaphor of hunting to describe her adaptive approach to solitary walking and sexual harassment: 'Having met so many predators, I learned to think like prey, as have most women' (242). The metaphor is picked up by Robyn Davidson when she scolds herself for not reacting more strongly to her bullying male boss Kurt: 'I hated myself for my infernal cowardice in dealing with people. It is such a female syndrome, so much the weakness of animals who have always been prey' (Davidson 1998, 15). In a literalisation of the metaphor, she later purchases a hunting rifle to frighten away unwanted male visitors to her lodgings in Alice Springs. A predatory patriarchy that seeks dominion over natural resources, animals and the bodies of women has instrumentalised movement as a form of expropriation (exploration and colonisation) and coercion (domestication of animals, confinement of women). The acceleration or blockage of movement become the two failsafe positions on the extractivist dial. The implication is that movement, as Marquis proclaims, becomes an important site of resistance but also that the notion of 'human' with respect to travel writing and the environment must be continuously qualified by considerations of gender, species awareness and socioeconomic situatedness.

Below Deck

Alexander von Humboldt, travel writer and naturalist, was clearly aware of this need for qualification when he identified the primary agents of climate change:

> When forests are destroyed, as they are everywhere in America by the European planters, with an imprudent precipitation, the springs are entirely dried up, or become less abundant. The beds of the rivers, remaining dry during a part of the year, are converted into torrents, whenever great rains fall on the heights. (von Humboldt 1814–29, 4/143–4)

He does not take refuge in the generalised abstraction of 'human'-induced climate change. The culprits are clear: 'European planters', a specific subset of humans. Humboldt's extensive travels laid the groundwork for his holistic view of climate, but the connections he made were not only between plant species and geological features in different parts of the world. In his *Political Essay on the Kingdom of New Spain* (1808–11) and *Political Essay on the Island of Cuba* (1826), Humboldt identifies the institution of slavery, the mistreatment of indigenous peoples and environmental destruction as part of a devastating continuum. Andrea Wulf reports how, back in his apartment in Berlin, Humboldt never tired of asking 'those who came from the United States about slavery and the oppression of Native Americans' (Wulf 2015, 276). He was particularly incensed when a pro-slavery publisher from the American South published an English translation of his *Political Essay on the Island of Cuba* with all the critical references to slavery removed. Humboldt's reaction was swift: '[o]utraged, Humboldt issued a press release that was published in newspapers across the United States, denouncing the edition and declaring that the deleted sections were the most important in the book' (277).

If Humboldt 'found connections everywhere', this has not always been true of his environmental successors. Malcom Ferdinand criticises the 'double fracture' where, on the one hand, environmental movements ignore the colonial legacy of slavery, racism and misogyny (Yousoff 2018) and, on the other, postcolonial movements are blind to the practices and consequences of environmental extractivism (Ferdinand 2019, 28). In trying to work through the ecological repercussions of slavery, Ferdinand uses the figurative language of travel. Starting with the slave ships that transport 12.5 million slaves from Africa to the Americas, he goes on to invoke the image of Noah's Ark, the spaceship of privilege that rescues the Chosen (White) Few from the ecological cataclysm to the *navire-monde* (world-ship), a Utopian vision of a racially just, ecologically sustainable coexistence among humans and between humans and the non-human (335). What the German scientist and the Caribbean critic share is a desire to make travel (and, by extension, travel writing) less opaque. In an ecological context, the wish is to reveal what the consequences of movement are and what makes voluntary and involuntary movement possible.

Fredric Jameson, in a discussion of Joseph Conrad's short novel *The Shadow-Line* (1916), speaks of the trauma experienced by a particular generation of seamen following the late nineteenth-century shift from sail to steam. The romance of wind and water gave way to the technocratic tyranny of boiler rooms and fossil fuels. What steam lacked in adventure, it more than made up for in capacity. Empire was the prime beneficiary. In Jameson's words: '[t]he steamboat facilitated the prodigious expansion of the British Empire ... the aquatic capillaries of world conquest' (Jameson 2020, 29). What the steamboat drives is the global spread of trade networks shadowing the capillary outreach of Empire. The elemental force of the wind is replaced by the technical abstraction of the boiler. The unwavering and invisible energy of coal succeeds the visible and dangerous energy of the tempest. In this new regime, the 'captain is now the locus of information' – technical information, that is – and the 'labourers have gone below the deck' (30) to tend the steam engines. For Jameson, Conrad's trauma, his yearning for the lost romance of the sea, points to a profound shift in economic focus from production to consumption:

> Marxian debates about value and immaterial labour are scarcely exotic or superfluous when they concern a system in which universal consumerism tends to conceal production in favour of distribution, a category that includes not only circulation and exchange as such, but also the full-blown ideology of communication and information that has become our dominant mode of understanding in a media society. (30)

The energy of fossil fuels makes labour increasingly invisible. What is lost from sight is the human-technical coupling that makes production possible. Of course, wind and water had little romance for those who preceded the labourers 'below the deck', namely, the African slaves who were transported to the Americas, or who, in at least 1.8 million cases, perished during the crossing (Ferdinand 2019, 227).

As Andrew Nikiforouk has pointed out, slave labour was a prime energy source from classical antiquity to the age of Empire (Nikiforouk 2012). Relatively few thinkers in the Western tradition, until recently (Mitchell 2011), have dwelt on the energy sources that power political, economic or social practices including, most conspicuously, travel, whether these sources were slaves or non-human forms of fuel. The slave or the steam engine rest in the realm of the unspoken or the unsaid. In other words, the close fit between racial discrimination, energy extraction and economic domination in the 'Plantationocene', to use Hathaway's and Ferdinand's term, means that travel gets largely written by the beneficiaries of these practices. This is mirrored in the overwhelmingly white nature of travel writing. When Colleen J. McElroy notes, in the closing years of the twentieth century, that '[a]ccounts of great travels never included black people, so I had no role models' (McElroy 1997, iv), she is describing a colour blindness that is borne out by the most cursory or the most thorough inspection of a travel writing section in a bookshop in the Anglophone world (see Youngs 2013, 115–30). Zora Neale Hurston, Maya Angelou, Richard Wright, Caryl Phillips, V. S. Naipaul and Noo Saro-Wiwa have all been distinguished contributors to the genre but their presence signals an even greater absence that is only slowly being remedied (Parker-Magyar 2020).

Pursuing the parallel between racial exclusion and environmental extractivism reveals an elitism of ends over means that has dogged the self-presentation of travel writing. Ludovic Hubler, in the epilogue to *The World by Hitchhiking* is explicit about what travel has meant to him: 'When I watch the national news broadcast, I am now able to look beyond the simple images of disasters with a better grasp of the underlying realities surrounding a news story and local life in the places covered' (Hubler 2016, 7568). Not uncharacteristically, he presents travel in terms of the ends it serves – combatting ignorance, prejudice, dogmatism – in much the same way as Francis Bacon did centuries earlier when declaring that travel 'in the younger sort, is a part of education, in the elder, a part of experience' (Bacon [1601] 2002, 374). Consensus about the ends of travel as enunciated by Hubler and Bacon is widespread. Slaves, hydrocarbons and nuclear power have the common property, however, of being means. Humans who have fixated on ends have often been reluctant to speak of means, subordinated to ends in a hierarchy of expressive value. By focusing on means, an ecocritical approach to travel writing can clarify where choices of mode, destination or representation are likely to lead, irrespective of the ends enunciated. In the words of Pascal Chabot, the aim of transitional thought – thought aimed at a transition to a carbon-neutral society – is to 'bring to light the invisible, reveal the hidden, understand what we consume so as not to become victims of what we consume' (Chabot 2015, 89).

Planet B

How the ends of travel conceal the means preoccupies Mark O'Connell as he analyses the rhetoric of those who see ecological collapse as a ticket to ride to

Elsewhere. O'Connell spent a year travelling to places from the Scottish Highlands to the Ukraine and New Zealand, 'landscapes both real and imaginary, where the end of the world could be glimpsed' (O'Connell 2020, 16). The aim of his apocalyptic Odyssey, in the shadow of the climate emergency, was to explore how particular groups of humans were preparing for planetary endgame. In 2018, in the summer of some of the worst wildfires in Californian history, O'Connell attended the twenty-first annual gathering of the Mars Society at the Pasadena Convention Center. He dutifully recorded the thoughts and convictions of those who believed not only that there would be much to write about on these new travels to other planets but also that there would be no choice but to try to go there. Stephen Hawking, the renowned physicist, up to the time of his death in 2018, was one of the most public champions of the backup planet thesis:

> I am convinced that humans need to leave Earth and make home on another planet. To stay risks annihilation. It could be an asteroid hitting the earth. It could be a new virus, climate change, nuclear war, or artificial intelligence gone rogue. For humans to survive I believe we must have the preparations in place within one hundred years. (Hawking 2018: 70)

Unlike climate activists who repeatedly argued there was no Planet B, the convention attendees believed that just such a planet existed. Its name was Mars. Noting that 'colonisation' was the term most often used to describe settling on Mars, O'Connell sees the frontier rhetoric around the planet as a further extension of an endlessly expansionist form of white American capitalism that projects fantasies of *terra nullius* into outer space.

Elon Musk, who had received the 'Mars Pioneer Award' at the 2012 Mars Society Convention, claimed that '[t]he United States is a distillation of the human spirit of exploration.' He went on to say that: '[a]lmost everyone here came from somewhere else. You couldn't ask for a group of people more interested in exploring the frontier' (cited in O'Connell 2020, 110). As O'Connell points out, Musk did not reference 'those who had been brought here against their will, or who had been here long before the frontier explorers he was invoking' (110). The language of extra-terrestrial travel is cast in terms of the noble end of exploration but the despoliation of ecological means back on earth (soil, air, water, non-human species) is passed over in silence. Indeed, Art Harman, a speaker at the Pasadena conference told his audience: 'You won't have the government, the EPA, saying you can't damage this or that endangered species. Not on Mars' (117). Environmental recklessness is condoned in a tragic repeat of the indifference that precipitated the climate catastrophe in the state where the convention was been held. Privatised space travel provides the environmental exit strategy for a vanishingly small number of billionaires, while the rest of humanity is left to slug it out on the abandoned planet, exhausted by the extractivist activities of the escapees (Spector and Higham 2019, 1–8).

Travel writing in *Notes from an Apocalypse* traces out not only the (historical, cultural, material) resource backdrop to the perverse utopias of interplanetary travel. It also points to sites of ecological devastation that provide a glimpse into a possible human future as much as they serve as a reminder of a neglectful political past. Moving through the depopulated landscapes of the Chernobyl Exclusion Zone, O'Connell observes:

> There was, I realized, a sense in which I was encountering the zone less as a site of real catastrophe, a barely conceivable tragedy of the very recent past, than as a vast diorama of an imagined future, a world in which humans had ceased entirely to exist. (212–13)

If travel writing, as we have known it thus far, has been a quintessentially human activity, then 'a world in which humans had ceased entirely to exist' would mean not just the end of human travel but the end of human travel writing. The excitable fantasies of delusional plutocrats, if realised, would ensure that travel writing would survive but at what unimaginable costs?

Visions of a Martian exodus are almost wholly a male concern and, for the cultural theorist Sarah Sharma, this is not especially surprising. Everyone is free to dream of exiting the tedious, the unpleasurable, the constraining, but when the rough gets tough, only one gender can, and classically does, leave the house to buy cigarettes: 'Exit is an exercise of patriarchal power, a privilege that occurs at the expense of cultivating and sustaining conditions of collective autonomy' (Sharma 2017). For women, Sharma argues, exit has only rarely been an option: 'Women's exit is hardly even on the table, given that women have historically been unable to choose when to leave or enter in inequitable power relations, let alone enter and exit in a carefree manner' (Sharma 2017). In opposition to a culture of exit is a culture of care 'which responds to the uncompromisingly tethered nature of human dependency and the contingency of life, the mutual precariousness of the human condition' (Sharma 2017). The culture of exit sees a resurgence (Brexit/Build the Wall) in periods when gender, race and ethnic privilege are threatened, precisely at the moment when a non-gendered culture of care is needed more than ever to ensure species survival. The allure of a culture of exit for travel writing is all too obvious. Indeed, one of the challenges for the genre is how to incorporate a culture of care into its practices and draw on writers and accounts that make this culture manifest, in the overall context of the climate emergency.

Connection

When Julian Hoffman travels to different locations on the planet, his problem is that some people care a great deal about the environment while others do not care at all. He has some sympathy for the indifferent. There can be a deadening abstraction, a cerebral vagueness around notions of species extinction and biodiversity loss. As Mark O'Connell confesses: 'I'm sick, in particular of climate change. Is it possible to be terrified and bored at the same time?' (O'Connell 2020, 7). For Hoffman, it is the experience of travel that rescues the climate question from abstract, well-meaning anxiety. Visiting Hoo Peninsula in the southeast of England, earmarked for destruction under a plan to extend Heathrow Airport, he becomes very quickly aware of what is at stake: 'Suddenly those losses in the larger landscape were made tangible for me. I could see in magnificent detail the lives that were endangered, belonging to the same communities of wild animals that had prompted the protective measures sheltering the area in the first place' (Hoffman 2019, 9). Travel brings him close to what is under threat, to what lies behind the screen of quantitative remoteness and beneath the percentages of perpetual crisis.

In the history of travel writing, there are, of course, troubling precedents for well-rehearsed concerns over imminent extinction. Commenting on writing about indigenous cultures, Tim Youngs notes that 'some of the narratives are redolent of salvage ethnography, with the air of preserving for us in the text lifeways that are about to disappear' (Youngs 2013, 184). Earlier, in his analysis of French travel literature in the twentieth century, Charles Forsdick had noted that the perceived decline of diversity was one of the most common preoccupations of the genre (Forsdick 2005, 3). What characterised the salvage ethnographers and the diversity undertakers was that they saw their role as largely archival, as registering the final hurrah of doomed cultures (Bongie 1991). Hoffman's perception of his role is radically different. He travels to record not the defeat of communities but their resurgence, to bear witness to their active fighting back against environmental disregard. There are no fey tableaux of cultural twilights. The mood is angry and active and Hoffman wants 'to explore loss in a way that wasn't simply elegiac but defiant' (13):

> Wherever I travelled, whether to ancient woodlands, urban meadows, coral reefs or relict prairies, I found people acutely aware of what loss looked like. For them it was neither abstract nor actuarial; it was real, visceral and imminent. (Hoffman 2019, 15)

A culture of care is, by definition, a culture of connection, but how does writing facilitate or impede particular kinds of connections? In speaking of the campaign to protect Hoo Peninsula from the bulldozer and wrecking ball, Hoffman claims that being mainly made of marshlands, places like the peninsula have 'largely been omitted from the map of aesthetic attention' (22). In travel writing and in painting, the conventions of Romantic art and the picaresque variously favoured well-tended pastures, valleys, lakes and mountain peaks. Other places and landscapes were relegated to the blank hinterland of the flat and the uninteresting. In working to reveal the 'magnificent detail' of the Hoo Peninsula, Hoffman has to work against an aesthetic bias that is partly a creation of the genre he practises.

There is, however, a more damaging bias in societies, and it has less to do with aesthetic preference and more to do with urban disconnection. Mark O'Connell, a city dweller, admits that, before his experiences in the Scottish Highlands, 'I was all for nature in theory, but in practice I had no feel for it, no sense of relationship with it at all' (O'Connell 2020, 148). As more and more of the world's population move to cities, the sense of remove from the natural environment can become increasingly pronounced, even though no city could function without water or a breathable atmosphere. This movement has been in train for quite some time and Romantic travel narratives and the objectification of nature were just some of the responses in populations that were increasingly distanced from their rural pasts (Smethurst 2013, 181).

Hoffman travels to North Kelvin Meadow in Glasgow, Scotland, and to Farm Terrace allotments in west Watford, England, to challenge the quarantining of ecology in the rural and the wilderness. Writing about North Kelvin Meadow, 1.4 hectares of urban space on the border between the West End of Glasgow and the Maryhill district, Hoffman argues that a 'small field of green in the middle of the city' had 'the ability to engage individuals deeply at every stage of life' (Hoffman 2019, 215). One particular stage of interest to Hoffman is childhood, and one of the areas in the Meadow is named the Children's Wood. What the green space offers the children in the city is an opportunity to play in and explore an area that is rich in organic life.

Robert Macfarlane had already noted in *Landmarks* the propensity for children in green spaces to develop a whole idiom and cartography of travel (Macfarlane 2015, 315–28). Hoffman wants to situate the environmental activism of the defenders of the urban Meadow in the fight against the extinction of childhood experience. By this, he means children growing up with less and less contact with the natural world. Hoffman refers to the work of Robert Michael Pyle, who charts the consequences of the cycle of disaffection beginning in childhood:

> As cities and metastasizing suburbs forsake their natural diversity, and their citizens grow more removed from personal contact with nature, awareness

and appreciation retreat. This breeds apathy toward environmental concerns
and, inevitably, further degradation of the common habitat. (Pyle 2011, 135)

In an urban version of vertical travel, it takes eleven-year-old Olive only 430
steps to circumnavigate the perimeter path of the Meadow, but within this space
there are endless pathways of environmental encounter and revelation. If a well-
documented fact is the dramatic loss of children's freedom to roam in urban
spaces (Macfarlane 2015, 323), then a commitment to explicit environmental
reconnection for children (we are always connected to environmental life-
support systems *in implicit ways*) means not only the possibility of a future
for our species but also a future for reading and writing about travel. There are
no travel writers on a dead planet. Travel writing can, of course, administer the
funeral rites to a dying planet through the elegiac evocation of lost Edens. What
should not be ignored, however, is the capacity of the genre, as detailed in these
pages, to quicken a sense of present responsibility for the climate crisis and
stimulate action into the future.

It has been something of a truism in travel writing that words fail in the
face of the natural sublime. Less remarked on, as was noted in Section 2, is
that words may make all the difference as to whether all we are left to
experience of the environmental sublime is abject terror. George Monbiot
commenting on the role of language in shaping our view of the natural world
begins with a biblical image: 'If Moses had promised the Israelites a land
flowing with mammary secretions and insect vomit, would they have fol-
lowed him into Canaan? Though this means milk and honey, I doubt it would
have inspired them' (Monbiot 2017). Monbiot finds the taxonomy of environmental protection – 'sites of special scientific interest', 'no-take zones',
'reference areas' – deeply alienating. Terms such as 'ecosystem services' and
'natural capital' are especially insidious as they imply that the natural world
is a 'resource' that solely exists to serve humans. Even a term such as
'climate change' confuses 'natural variation with the catastrophic disruption
we cause; a confusion deliberately exploited by those who deny our role'
(Monbiot 2017). Although cognitive linguists, social psychologists and the
advertising industry agree that words shape how we view reality, Monbiot
wonders why 'those who seek to protect the living planet – and who were
doubtless inspired to devote their lives to it through the same sense of wonder
and reverence – so woefully fail to capture these values in the way they name
the world?' He wants to recruit 'poets and cognitive linguists and amateur
nature lovers' in this transformative project of redescription, but he might
equally have added travel writers to this redemptive list. Travel writers have
been engaging for centuries with the natural world, albeit with radically

different motives. If some of these writers have contributed to a petrified museum order, a distanced and objectified view of the planet, others have drawn readers' attention repeatedly to the 'enchantment', 'delight' and 'awe' that Monbiot sees as essential to a new language for the natural world. It is precisely this capacity of language to capture joy in 'corners of common greenery' that enlivens Hoffman's travels through urban environments, 'a blue butterfly bringing a radiant smile to a young girl's face by landing on her hand, an old man lifting from the earth the first fresh carrots of the year, a Finnish summer song in a Scottish stand of silver birch' (Hoffman 2019, 248). If words are all that travel writers have, Monbiot's contention is that they are the most powerful and most neglected of tools in resisting the cycle of disaffection and ecological collapse.

One word that is in itself problematic is 'environment' – 'an empty word that creates no pictures in the mind' (Monbiot 2017). The suggestion is of something that surrounds us, present but discrete and apart. As the climate crisis makes evident, this is a dangerous illusion; humans are in and not apart from 'nature'. A failure, by very powerful humans, to acknowledge this fact, has dramatically aggravated environmental breakdown. In advocating for 'more-than-human' histories, Emily O'Gorman and Andrea Gaynor claim that more-than-human is 'not a synonym for "nature" or the "nonhuman" but, rather, a term that highlights the primacy of relations over entities (including the "human")' (O'Gorman and Gaynor 2020, 7). The basic principle here is 'co-constitution – that organisms, elements and forces cannot be considered in isolation but must always be considered in relation' (717). There is no external 'nature' or 'environment' with which humans interact. They are always, already, involved in the 'more-than-human'. It is not a question of demonstrating that 'the "natural" is really "cultural" or to reassert a biophysical reality' (724) but of recognising the full range of participants in the more-than-human world of multispecies coexistence and non-human entanglements. In the case of animals, for example, Catherine Johnston makes the case for a 'responsible anthropomorphism' as:

> [A] way of knowing about and knowing with animals not based on our shared sentience, our shared place in the world or any other such abstract philosophical argument, but on our actual relationships, our day-to-day living and working. (Johnston 2008, 646)

The term 'more-than-human world' was coined by David Abram in his *Spell of the Sensuous*, a work based on a consideration of indigenous ontologies (Abram 1997). The long tradition of indigenous travel, more often the subject of orature than literature, provides a glimpse into post-anthropocentric modes of travelling, a negotiation of a world teeming with non-human presence that demands recognition and reciprocity (Coates 2004, 25–64; Clarke 2018, 49–61). Emerging writers such as Ursula Pike in *An Indian among los Indígenas: A Native Travel Memoir* (2021) are drawing attention to exclusion of indigenous perspectives from modes of travel reporting. Robin Wall Kimmerer, the writer, botanist and citizen of the Potawatomi Nation, has called for a 'grammar of animacy' as a way of acknowledging kinship with plants, mountains and lakes. A challenge for indigenous writers is how to 'recreate a new relationship with the natural world when it's not the same as the natural world your tribal community had a longstanding relationship with' (Yeh 2020).

In the age of the Anthropocene, the new relationship with the natural world is the lot of all humanity. When the very modes of travel contribute actively to the end of the possibility of travel, then travel writing has to reflect not so much on the end as on the ends and means of travel. How humans travel, which humans get to travel, how travel promotes or makes legible a 'grammar of intimacy' – these are all central questions for writing about journeying in the age of the Anthropocene. Edgar Degas, writing in 1886, declared that '[n]othing in art must look like an accident, even movement' (cited in Barnes 2020, 6). Thinking purposefully about what travel writing can do in a climate emergency is about avoiding the accidents, maintaining the more-than-human movement, the movement towards life rather than death.

References

Abram, David. 1997. *The Spell of the Sensuous: Perception and Language in a More-Than-Human World*. London: Vintage.

Almond, R.E.A., M. Grooten and T. Petersen. 2020. *WWF (2020) Living Planet Report 2020: Bending the Curve of Biodiversity Loss – Summary*. Gland: WWF.

Arendt, Hannah. 1958. *The Human Condition*, 2nd ed. Chicago: Chicago University Press.

Augé, Marc. 2002. *In the Metro*, trans. Tom Conley. Minneapolis, MN: University of Minnesota Press.

Bacon, Francis. 2002. 'Of Travel' [1601]. In *The Major Works*, ed. Brian Vickers, 374–6. Oxford: Oxford University Press.

Barnes, Julian. 2020. 'Summarising Oneself'. *London Review of Books* 42 (22): 5–8.

Becker, Elizabeth. 2013. 'Is Tourism the Most Destructive Enterprise?' *YaleGlobal Online*. https://yaleglobal.yale.edu/content/tourism-most-destructive-enterprise.

Bennett, Jane. 2010. *Vibrant Matter: A Political Ecology of Things*. Durham, NC: Duke University Press.

Berdynk, Luda. 2019. 'Does the Ethical Tourist Really Exist?' https://mahb.stanford.edu/whats-happening/ethical-tourist-really-exist.

Bertrand, Romain. 2019. *Le détail du monde: l'art perdu de la description de la nature*. Paris: Seuil.

Blessington, Marguerite. 1822. *A Tour in the Isle of Wight, in the Autumn of 1820*. London: A&R Spottiswoode.

Blessington, Marguerite. 1839–40. *The Idler in Italy*. Three vols. London: Henry Colburn.

Blessington, Marguerite. 1841. *The Idler in France*. Paris: Baudry.

Bongie, Christopher. 1991. *Exotic Memories: Literature, Colonialism and the Fin de Siècle*. Stanford, CA: Stanford University Press.

Bonneuil, Christophe and Jean-Baptiste Fressoz. 2016. *The Shock of the Anthropocene: The Earth, History and Us*, trans. David Fernbach. London: Verso.

Braidotti, Rosi. 2013. *The Posthuman*. Cambridge: Polity.

Burke, Edmund. 1767. *A Philosophical Inquiry into the Origin of our Ideas of the Sublime and Beautiful* [1757], 5th ed. London: Dodsley.

Butler, Eoin. 2020. 'Nowhere'. *The Irish Times*, 26 September.

Buzard, James. 1993. *The Beaten Track: European Tourism, Literature, and the Ways to 'Culture', 1800–1918*. Oxford: Oxford University Press.

Byerly, Alison. 2012. *Are We There Yet? Virtual Travel and Victorian Realism*. Ann Arbor: University of Michigan Press.

Chabot, Pascal. 2015. *L'Âge des transitions*. Paris: PUF.

Chakrabarty, Dipesh. 2009. 'The Climate of History: Four Theses'. *Critical Inquiry* 35 (2): 197–222.

Chan, Angela. 2020. 'Is Virtual Travel Here to Stay Even After the Pandemic Subsides? 'www.nationalgeographic.com/travel/2020/04/can-virtual-real ity-replace-real-tourism-during-pandemic-and-beyond.

Clarke, Robert. 2018. 'History, Memory and Trauma in Postcolonial Travel Writing'. In *The Cambridge Companion to Postcolonial Travel Writing*, ed. Robert Clarke, 49–61. Cambridge: Cambridge University Press.

Coates, Ken S. 2004. *A Global History of Indigenous Peoples*. London: Palgrave Macmillan.

Coates, Peter. 1998. *Nature: Western Attitudes since Ancient Times*. Oxford: Polity.

Coleman, Mat and Kathryn Yusoff. 2014. 'Interview with Elizabeth Povinelli'. http://societyandspace.com/2014/03/06/interview-with-elizabeth-povinelli-with-mat-coleman-and-kathryn-yusoff.

Crane, Kylie. 2019. 'Ecocriticism and Travel'. In *The Cambridge History of Travel Writing*, eds. Nandini Das and Tim Youngs, 535–49. Cambridge: Cambridge University Press.

Cronin, Michael. 2000. *Across the Lines: Travel, Language, Translation*. Cork: Cork University Press.

Danowski, Deborah and Eduardo Viveiros de Castro. 2014. 'L'Arrêt de monde'. In *De l'univers clos au monde infini*, ed. Émilie Hache, 221–339. Bellevaux: Éditions Dehors.

Daston, Lorraine. 1992. 'Objectivity and the Escape from Perspective'. *Social Studies of Science* 22 (4): 597–618.

Davidson, Robyn. 1998. *Tracks* [1980]. London: Picador.

Davis, Diana K. 2011. 'Imperialism, Orientalism, and the Environment in the Middle East'. In *Environmental Imaginaries of the Middle East and North Africa*, eds. Diana K. Davis and Edmund Burke, 1–22. Athens: Ohio University Press.

De Botton, Alain. 2009. *A Week at the Airport: A Heathrow Diary*. London: Profile.

De Decker, Kris. 2015. 'Why We Need a Speed Limit for the Internet'. *Low Tech Magazine*. www.lowtechmagazine.com/2015/10/can-the-internet-run-on-renewable-energy.html.

De Esquivel, Diego. 1905. 'Relación de Chinantha'. In *Papels del Nueva España*, ed. Francisco del Paso y Tronocosco, 56–68. Vol. 4. Madrid.

Descartes, René. 1968. *Discourse on Method and the Meditations*, trans. F. E. Sutcliffe. London: Penguin.

Edwards, Justin D. and Rune Graulund. 2012. *Mobility at Large: Globalization, Textuality and Innovative Travel Writing*. Liverpool: Liverpool University Press.

Elsner, Jás and Joan-Pau Rubiés, eds. 1999. *Voyages and Visions: Towards a Cultural History of Travel*. London: Reaktion.

Ferdinand, Malcom. 2019. *Une écologie décoloniale: penser l'écologie depuis le monde caribéen*. Paris: Seuil.

Fletcher, Robert. 2019. 'Ecotourism After Nature: Anthropocene Tourism as a New Capitalist "Fix"'. *Journal of Sustainable Tourism* 27 (3): 522–35.

Forsdick, Charles. 2005. *Travel in Twentieth-Century French and Francophone Cultures: The Persistence of Diversity*. Oxford: Oxford University Press.

Forsdick, Charles. 2020. 'Vertical Travel'. In *The Routledge Research Companion to Travel Writing*, eds. Alasdair Pettinger and Tim Youngs, 99–112. London: Routledge.

Fussell, Paul. 1980. *Abroad: British Literary Travelling Between the Two World Wars*. Oxford: Oxford University Press.

Ganatra, Shilpa, Manchán Magan, Darragh Geraghty, Jamie Ball and Sandra O'Connell. 2020. 'Travelling Without Moving'. *The Irish Times*, 11 April.

Garry, John. 2020. 'Why Virtual Tours are Here to Stay'. *Lonely Planet*, 14 July. www.lonelyplanet.com/articles/virtual-tours-here-to-stay.

Graulund, Rune. 2016. 'Writing Travel in the Anthropocene: Disastrous Life at the End of the Arctic'. *Studies in Travel Writing* 20 (3): 285–95.

Graulund, Rune. 2019. 'End-of-Travel'. In *Keywords for Travel Writing Studies*, eds. Charles Forsdick, Kathryn Walchester and Zoë Kinsley, 271–8. London: Anthem. E-book.

Greenblatt, Stephen. 2012. *The Swerve: How the Renaissance Began*. London: Vintage.

Gregory, Richard L. 1984. *Mind in Science: A History of Explanations in Psychology and Physics*. Harmondsworth: Penguin.

Grove, Richard H. 1995. *Green Imperialism: Colonial Expansion, Tropical Island Edens and the Origins of Environmentalism, 1600–1860*. Cambridge: Cambridge University Press.

Haraway, Donna. 2015. 'Anthropocene, Capitalocene, Plantationocene, Chthulucene: Making Kin'. *Environmental Humanities* 6: 159–65.

Harman, Graham. 2018. *Object-Oriented Ontology: A New Theory of Everything*. London: Pelican.

Heidegger, Martin. 1977. *The Question Concerning Technology and Other Essays*, trans. William Lovitt. New York: Harper.

Hoffman, Julian. 2019. *Irreplaceable: The Fight to Save our Wild Places*. London: Penguin.

Holy Bible: Chain Reference Edition. 1984. Oxford: Oxford University Press.

Horowitz, Alexandra. 2013. *On Looking: Eleven Walks with Expert Eyes*, New York: Scribner.

Hubler, Ludovic. 2016. *The World by Hitchhiking: Five Years at the University of Life*. Kindle.

Ingold, Tim. 2000. *The Perception of the Environment: Essays in Livelihood, Dwelling and Skill*. London: Routledge.

Irfan, Umair. 2019. 'Air Travel Is a Huge Contributor to Climate Change. A New Global Movement Wants to Be Ashamed to Fly'. *Vox*, 30 November. www.vox.com/the-highlight/2019/7/25/8881364/greta-thunberg-climate-change-flying-airline.

Jameson, Fredric. 2020. 'Time and the Sea'. *London Review of Books* 42 (8): 29–30.

Jamie, Kathleen. 2012. *Sightlines*. London: Sort Of Books.

Jarvis, Robin. 2012. *Romantic Readers and Transatlantic Travel: Expeditions and Tours in North America, 1760–1840*. Farnham, UK: Ashgate.

Jencks, Charles. 2005. 'Nature Talking with Nature'. In *Return to Postmodernism: Theory – Travel Writing – Autobiography*, ed. Klaus Stierstorfer, 389–95. Heidelberg: Winter Verlag.

John of Pian de Carpini. 1929. 'The Journey of Friar John of Pian de Carpini to the Court of Kuyuk Khan 1245–1247 as Narrated by Himself'. In *Contemporaries of Marco Polo*, ed. Manuel Komroff, 27–71. London: Cape.

Johnston, Catherine. 2008. 'Beyond the Clearing: Towards a Dwelt Animal Geography'. *Progress in Human Geography* 32 (5): 633–49.

Kelly, Matthew, ed. 2019. *Nature and the Environment in Nineteenth-Century Ireland*. Liverpool: Liverpool University Press.

Kindersley, [Jemima]. 1777. *Letters from the Island of Teneriffe, Brazil, the Cape of Good Hope and the East Indies*. London: Nourse.

Klein, Naomi. 2014. *This Changes Everything: Capitalism vs. the Climate*. London: Allen Lane.

Klein, Naomi. 2019. *On Fire: The Burning Case for a Green New Deal*. London: Penguin.

Laybourn-Langton, Laurie, Lesley Rankin and Darren Baxter. 2019. *This is a Crisis: Facing Up to the Age of Environmental Breakdown*. London: Institute for Public Policy Research.

Leask, Nigel. 2002. *Curiosity and the Aesthetics of Travel Writing, 1770–1840: 'From an Antique Land'*. Oxford: Oxford University Press.

Lee, Debbie. 2019. 'Travelling in Wilderness'. In *The Cambridge History of Travel Writing*, eds. Nandini Das and Tim Youngs, 376–90. Cambridge: Cambridge University Press.

Levin, David Michael, ed. 1993. *Modernity and the Hegemony of Vision*. Berkeley: University of California Press.

Ley, Charles David, ed. 1947. *Portuguese Voyages 1498–1663*. London: Dent.

Lipska, Aneta. 2017. *The Travel Writings of Marguerite Blessington: The Most Gorgeous Lady on Tour*. London: Anthem.

Locke, John. 1704. *A Collection of Voyages and Travels*, ed. Awnsham. London: John Churchill.

Lopez, Barry. 2014. *Arctic Dreams* [1986]. London: Vintage.

Macfarlane, Robert. 2015. *Landmarks*. London: Hamish Hamilton.

Macfarlane, Robert. 2019. *Underland: A Deep Time Journey*. London: Penguin.

Magan, Manchán. 2020. 'Coming Back to Earth'. *The Irish Times*, 25 January.

Marquis, Sarah. 2016. *Wild by Nature: From Siberia to Australia, Three Years Alone in the Wilderness on Foot*. London: Allen & Unwin.

Mason, Jason, ed. 2016. *Anthropocene or Capitalocene? Nature, History and the Crisis of Capitalism*. New York: PM Press.

McClanahan, Paige and Debra Karim. 2020. '52 Places, Virtually'. *New York Times*, 14 April. www.nytimes.com/2020/04/14/travel/52-places-to-go-vir tual-travel.html.

McElroy, Colleen J. 1997. *A Long Way from St. Louie*. Minneapolis, MN: Coffee House Press.

McIntosh, Alastair. 2002. *Soil and Soul: People versus Corporate Power*. London: Aurum.

McKibben, Bill. 1989. *The End of Nature*. New York: Anchor.

Melville, Hermann. 1967. *Moby-Dick or, the Whale* [1851]. New York: W.W. Norton.

Mitchell, Timothy. 2011. *Carbon Democracy: Political Power in the Age of Oil*. London: Verso.

Monbiot, George. 2006. *Heat: How to Stop the Planet Burning*. London: Penguin.

Monbiot, George. 2017. 'Forget "the Environment": We Need New Words to Convey Life's Wonders'. *The Guardian*, 9 August. www.theguardian.com/

commentisfree/2017/aug/09/forget-the-environment-new-words-lifes-won
ders-language.

Moore, Jason. 2015. *Capitalism in the Web of Life: Ecology and the Accumulation of Capital*. London: Verso.

Morton, Timothy. 2018. *Being Ecological*. London: Pelican.

Nikiforuk, Andrew. 2014. *The Energy of Slaves: Oil and the New Servitude*. Vancouver: Greystone.

O'Connell, Mark. 2020. *Notes from an Apocalypse: A Personal Journey to the End of the World and Back*. London: Granta.

O'Gorman, Emily and Andrea Gaynor. 2020. 'More-Than-Human Histories'. *Environmental History* 25 (4): 711–35.

Ong, Walter J. 2012. *Orality and Literacy*, 3rd ed. London: Routledge.

Organisation of Economic Cooperation and Development (OECD). 2020. 'Covid-19 and the Aviation Industry: Impact and Policy Responses'. https://read.oecd-ilibrary.org/view/?ref=137_137248-fyhl0sbu89&title=COVID-19-and-the-aviation-industry.

Osborn, Fairfield. 1948. *Our Plundered Planet*. Boston: Little, Brown & Company.

Parker-Magyar, Katherine. 2020. '15 Black Travel Writers to Read Now'. *Forbes*, 21 July. www.forbes.com/sites/katherineparkermagyar/2020/07/21/15-black-travel-writers-to-read-now/?sh=4346c75f7637.

Perec, Georges. 1982. *Tentative d'épuisement d'un lieu parisien*. Paris: Bourgois.

Perec, Georges. 1989. *L'infra-ordinaire*. Paris: Seuil.

Pettinger, Alasdair. 2019. 'Vertical Travel'. In *Keywords for Travel Writing Studies*, eds. Charles Forsdick, Kathryn Walchester and Zoë Kinsley, 796–802. London: Anthem. E-book.

Pike, Ursula. 2021. *An Indian Among Los Indígenas: A Native Travel Memoir*. Nanaimo, BC: Strong Nations Publishing.

Pleumarom, Anita and Chee Yoke Ling. 2017. 'Tinkering with "Ecotourism" Hides the Real Face of Tourism'. www.travindy.com/2017/05/tinkering-with-ecotourism-hides-the-real-face-of-tourism.

Plumwood, Val. 1993. *Feminism and the Mastery of Nature*. London: Routledge.

Plumwood, Val. 2007. 'Human Exceptionalism and the Limitations of Animals: A Review of Raimond Gaita's *The Philosopher's Dog*'. *Australian Humanities Review*, August. http://australianhumanitiesreview.org/archive/Issue-August-2007/EcoHumanities/Plumwood.html.

Plumwood, Val. 2009. 'Nature in the Active Voice'. *Australian Humanities Review* 46. http://australianhumanitiesreview.org/2009/05/01/nature-in-the-active-voice.

Pratt, Mary-Louise. 1992. *Imperial Eyes: Travel Writing and Transculturation.* London: Routledge.

Pyle, Robert Michael. 2011. *The Thunder Tree: Lessons from an Urban Wildland.* Corvallis, OR: Oregon State University Press.

Raleigh, Walter. 1848. *Discoverie of the Large, Rich and Beautiful Empire of Guyana* [1596]. London: Hakluyt Society.

Robinson, Mary. 2019. *Climate Justice.* London: Bloomsbury.

Roorda, Randall. 2001. 'Deep Maps in Eco-Literature'. *Michigan Quarterly Review* 40 (1): 259–72.

Rose, Deborah Bird. 2013. 'Val Plumwood's Philosophical Animism: Attentive Interactions in the Sentient World' *Environmental Humanities* 3: 93–109.

Roser, Max. 2020. 'Tourism'. 'Our World in Data'. https://ourworldindata.org/tourism#empirical-view.

Rumiz, Paolo. 2015. *The Fault Line: Travelling the Other Europe, from Finland to Ukraine*, tTrans. Gregory Conti. New York: Rizzoli Ex Libris.

Saro-Wiwa, Noo. 2013. *Looking for Transwonderland: Travels in Nigeria.* London: Granta.

Secord, James. 2006. 'How Scientific Conversation Became Shop Talk'. *Transactions of the Royal Historical Society* 17: 129–56.

Sharma, Sarah. 2017. 'Exit and the Extensions of Man'. *transmediale*, 8 May. https://transmediale.de/content/exit-and-the-extensions-of-man.

Sherringham, Michael. 2006. *Everyday Life: Theories and Practices from Surrealism to the Present.* Oxford: Oxford University Press.

Smethurst, Paul. 2013. *Travel Writing and the Natural World 1760–1840.* Basingstoke: Palgrave Macmillan.

Snowden, Frank M. 2020. *Epidemics and Society: From the Black Death to the Present.* London: Yale University Press.

Solnit, Rebecca. 2014. *Wanderlust: A History of Walking.* London: Granta.

Soper, Kate. 1995. *What is Nature?* Oxford: Blackwell.

Spector, Sam and James E. S. Higham. 2019. 'Space Tourism in the Anthropocene'. *Annals of Tourism Research* 79 (C): 1–8.

Sterne, Laurence. 1892. *A Sentimental Journey through France and Italy* [1768]. London: George Price.

Stiegler, Bernd. 2013. *Traveling in Place: A History of Armchair Travel*, trans. Peter Filkins. Chicago: Chicago University Press.

Szerszynski, Bronislaw and John Urry. 2006. 'Visuality, Mobility and the Cosmopolitan: Inhabiting the World From Afar'. *British Journal of Sociology* 57 (1): 113–31.

Taylor, Charles. 1995. *Philosophical Arguments.* Cambridge, MA: Harvard University Press.

Tesson, Sylvain. 2019. *La panthère des neiges*. Paris: Gallimard.

Thomas, Keith. 1984. *Man and the Natural World: Changing Attitudes in England 1500–1800*. London: Penguin.

Thompson, Carl. 2017. 'Journeys to Authority: Reassessing Women's Early Travel Writing, 1763–1862'. *Women's Writing* 24 (2): 131–50.

Timperley, Jocelyn. 2017. 'Explainer: The Challenge of Tackling Aviation's Non-CO_2 Emissions'. *Carbon Brief*, 15 March 2015. www.carbonbrief.org/explainer-challenge-tackling-aviations-non-co2-emissions.

Topping, Margaret. 2019. 'Virtual Travel'. In *Keywords for Travel Writing Studies*, ed. Charles Forsdick, Kathryn Walchester and Zoë Kinsley, 803–7. London: Anthem. (E-book.)

Turner, James. 2014. *Philology: The Forgotten Origins of the Modern Humanities*. Princeton NJ: Princeton University Press.

Turner, Katherine. 2001. *British Travellers in Europe: Authorship, Gender and National Identity*. Aldershot: Ashgate.

Urbain, Jean-Didier. 1998. *Secrets de voyage: menteurs, imposteurs et autres voyageurs immédiats*. Paris: Payot.

Urry, John and Jonas Larsen. 2011. *The Tourist Gaze 3.0*, 3rd ed. London: Sage.

Virilio, Paul. 2010. *The Futurism of the Instant: Stop-Eject*, trans. Julie Rose. Oxford: Polity.

Vogt, William. 1948. *Road to Survival*. New York: William Sloane.

Von Humboldt, Alexander. 1814–1829. *Personal Narrative of Travels to the Equinoctial Regions of the New Continent during the years 1799–1804*, trans. Helen Maria Williams. London: Longman, Hurst, Rees, Orme, Brown and John Murray.

Wilde, Jane. 1893. *Social Studies*. London: Ward & Downey.

Wilson, Edward O. 2003. *The Future of Life*. London: Abacus.

Wulf, Andrea. 2015. *The Invention of Nature: The Adventures of Alexander von Humboldt, the Lost Hero of Science*. London: John Murray.

Yeh, James. 2020. 'Robin Wall Kimmerer: People Can't Understand the World as a Gift Unless Someone Shows Them How'. *The Guardian*, 23 May. www.theguardian.com/books/2020/may/23/robin-wall-kimmerer-people-cant-understand-the-world-as-a-gift-unless-someone-shows-them-how.

Youngs, Tim. 2013. *The Cambridge Introduction to Travel Writing*. Cambridge: Cambridge University Press.

Yousoff, Kathryn. 2018. *A Billion Black Anthropocenes or None*. Minneapolis, MN: University of Minnesota Press.

For Trish, for everything

Cambridge Elements

Travel Writing

Nandini Das
University of Oxford
Nandini Das is a literary scholar and cultural historian, Professor of Early Modern Literature and Culture at the University of Oxford, and Fellow of Exeter College, Oxford. With Tim Youngs, she has co-edited *The Cambridge History of Travel Writing* (2019), and published widely on early modern English literature, cross-cultural encounters, and travel accounts.

Tim Youngs
Nottingham Trent University
Tim Youngs is Professor of English and Travel Studies at Nottingham Trent University. His books include *The Cambridge Companion to Travel Writing* (edited with Peter Hulme, 2002), *The Cambridge Introduction to Travel Writing* (2013), and *The Cambridge History of Travel Writing* (edited with Nandini Das, 2019). He edits the journal *Studies in Travel Writing*.

About the Series
Travel writing is enormously varied. It consists of several different forms and has a long history across many cultures. This series aims to reflect that diversity, offering exciting studies of a range of travel texts and topics. The Elements further advance the latest thinking in travel writing, extending previous work and opening up the field to fresh readings and subjects of inquiry.

Cambridge Elements ☰

Travel Writing

Elements in the Series

Eco-Travel: Journeying in the Age of the Anthropocene
Michael Cronin

A full series listing is available at: www.cambridge.org/ELTW

Printed in the United States
by Baker & Taylor Publisher Services